Historical American Biographies

HENRY FORD

Building Cars for Everyone

Pat McCarthy

Enslow Publishers, Inc.

40 Industrial Road   PO Box 38
Box 398   Aldershot
Berkeley Heights, NJ 07922   Hants GU12 6BP
USA   UK

http://www.enslow.com

Dedication

*To my nephew and his wife, Tim and Tina Ullery,
and their children, Heather and Adam, with thanks
for always being there for me when I need them.*
—Aunt Pat

Copyright © 2002 by Pat McCarthy

Library of Congress Cataloging-in-Publication Data

McCarthy, Pat, 1940–
    Henry Ford : building cars for everyone / Pat McCarthy.
       p. cm. — (Historical American biographies)
    Includes bibliographical references and index.
    Summary: A biography of the American inventor and industrialist who
is best known for making the automobile practical, through both his
revolutionary assembly lines and his desire to make a car every working
man could afford.
    ISBN 0-7660-1620-X
    1. Ford, Henry, 1863–1947—Juvenile literature. 2. Industrialists—
United States—Biography—Juvenile literature. 3. Automobile industry
and trade—United States—Biography—Juvenile literature. 4. Automobile
engineers—United States—Biography—Juvenile literature. [1. Ford,
Henry, 1863–1947. 2. Automobile industry and trade. 3. Industrialists.]
I. Title. II. Series.
    TL140.F6 M33 2002
    338.76292'092—dc21
                                 2001006693

Printed in the United States of America

10 9 8 7 6 5 4 3 2

To Our Readers:
We have done our best to make sure all Internet addresses in this book
were active and appropriate when we went to press. However, the
author and the publisher have no control over and assume no liability
for the material available on those Internet sites or on other Web sites
they may link to. Any comments or suggestions can be sent by e-mail to
comments@enslow.com or to the address on the back cover.

Illustration Credits: Courtesy of Ford Motor Company, pp. 7, 12, 18,
32, 37, 40, 43, 46, 53, 59, 67, 71, 84, 98, 109; Enslow Publishers, Inc.,
p. 21; Photos taken at Greenfield Village by Pat McCarthy © 2000,
pp. 9, 35; Reproduced from the Collections of the Library of Congress,
p. 4.

Cover Illustration: © Corel Corporation (Background); Reproduced
from the Collections of the Library of Congress (Ford Portrait).

CONTENTS

Henry Ford

1

TESTING THE QUADRICYCLE

It was the middle of a rainy Detroit night on June 4, 1896, and thirty-three-year-old Henry Ford was excited. His horseless carriage, which he called the Quadricycle, was finally finished.[1] He and his friend Jim Bishop had worked hard on it for months.

The vehicle had four bicycle wheels, held together by a flimsy frame, with a bicycle seat mounted in the middle. A long curved wooden tiller was used to steer the vehicle. A button on the end of the tiller was connected to a doorbell, in case the driver had to warn people to get out of the way.

As Ford got ready to take the Quadricycle out of the shed where he had built it, he realized his invention was too big to fit through the door. He grabbed an ax and knocked bricks out of the wall next to the door. Nothing could stop him now. He cleared away the debris, and he and Bishop pushed the car into the alley.

As his wife, Clara, watched, Ford put the clutch in neutral and spun the flywheel. The motor sputtered to life, shaking the light framework of the body. He hopped onto the vibrating seat, shifted into low gear, and off he went, bumping down the cobblestone alley with Bishop following on his bicycle.

Ford was so excited that the Quadricycle actually worked that he did not mind the rain. At the end of the alley, he turned onto Grand River Avenue and drove to Washington Boulevard. The car came to a sudden stop in front of the Cadillac Hotel in downtown Detroit. A group of merrymakers came out and gathered around the car, curious to see what it was.[2]

Ford and Bishop hurried to the nearby Edison Illuminating Company where they worked and got a spring to replace the broken one. They easily fixed the car, then Ford chugged back home. At less than seven hundred pounds, the Quadricycle weighed less and was faster than any other car. It had a two-cylinder engine, four horsepower, and two speeds.

Henry Ford sits in his Quadricycle. Ford took his first ride in the invention in the pouring rain.

In low gear it would go ten miles per hour, and in high it could get up to twenty. There was no reverse.

Few people saw the Quadricycle that night, and its debut was not reported in the Detroit newspapers. Henry Ford was satisfied to know that it ran, and immediately set about making improvements.

The next morning, he hired two coworkers, who were bricklayers, to repair the wall. When Ford's landlord came by to collect the rent, he was furious about the mess. Ford told him he had to knock the wall down to get the Quadricycle out. When the man heard the vehicle actually ran, he began excitedly asking questions. He suggested they not replace the bricks, but put swinging doors on the opening of the shed so they could move the vehicle in and out. This may have been the first garage door in the United States.[3]

2

HENRY FORD, FARM BOY

In the upstairs bedroom over the parlor, a boy was born to William and Mary Ford. Their first baby had died at birth the year before, so they were especially pleased to have a healthy child. They named him Henry, for William's brother.

It was July 30, 1863, in the middle of the Civil War. The Fords lived on a ninety-acre farm in Dearbornville, Michigan. William Ford's family had come from Ireland during the Potato Famine in 1847. During the famine, many Irish people were starving because the potato crop, their main source of food, had failed due to disease. They were English, but had been farming in Ireland.

Henry Ford was born in the upstairs parlor of this farmhouse on July 30, 1863.

William's father, John Ford, left Ireland with his wife, Thomasina, and their seven children. Thomasina died on the way and was buried at sea. The Fords went directly to Dearbornville, where John's two brothers lived. William, the oldest son, helped his father clear the land.

In the late 1850s, William worked for a neighbor, Patrick O'Hern. The O'Herns had adopted a little girl, Mary Litogot, when her father was killed in a fall. She was fourteen years younger than William Ford, but in 1861 they were married.

William was handsome, with curly hair and beard and clear eyes. Mary was an attractive girl with brown hair and dark eyes.[1]

William Ford ran a profitable farm, with horses and sheep, a wood lot, and a small orchard. He did carpentry work, too. He served on the school board and as road commissioner, vestryman in the village church, and master of the Dearborn Lodge.

The farmhouse was on the line between two townships. It was said that Henry went to bed in Dearborn Township and ate breakfast in Springwells Township.[2]

Henry grew up on the farm, but the rural society was giving way to an industrial society. Freighters

Bird-watching

Henry's father introduced him to nature at an early age and he quickly developed a lifelong love of birds. "The first thing I remember in my life," he said later, "is my father taking my brother [John] and myself to see a bird's nest under a large oak. I remember the nest with four eggs and also the bird and hearing its song."[3] He later learned that it was a song sparrow. He even recalled his father turning the plow aside to avoid running over a bird's nest. He gave his grandfather O'Hern credit for teaching him the names of many birds, including the red-headed woodpecker, swallow, bluebird, and robin.[4] When Henry grew up, he could identify most birds by their calls, and had hundreds of birdhouses on his estate.

constantly went up and down the river with raw materials for the many small mills, factories, and machine shops springing up in nearby Detroit.

Henry was soon joined by five brothers and sisters, John, Margaret, Jane, William, and Robert.

Henry idolized his mother. He remembered the advice she gave him about work. He recalled,

> She taught me that disagreeable jobs call for courage and patience and self-discipline, and she taught me also that "I don't want to" gets a fellow nowhere . . . My mother used to say, when I grumbled about it, "Life will give you many unpleasant tasks to do; your duty will be hard and disagreeable and painful to you at times, but you must do it. You may have pity on others, but you must not pity yourself."[5]

On January 11, 1871, seven-year-old Henry walked the mile and a half to the Scotch Settlement School to begin his education. His mother had already taught him to read. The red brick school with glass windows and a stove was quite modern for that day. The children sat in double desks facing the teacher's desk, which was on a platform at the front of the room. The teacher taught all eight grades in one room.

In the winter, there was often a male teacher, but he was replaced by a woman in the spring when it was time to plant crops. Henry's first teacher was a young girl named Emilie Nardin, who boarded with the Fords.[6]

As a boy, Henry Ford was very close to his mother, who taught him how to read before he even started school.

Henry read from the McGuffey *Readers*, which contained poems and stories stressing moral values. He read well enough, and was good at arithmetic, but never learned to spell very well. His best friend was Edsel Ruddiman, the brightest boy in the class. The two managed to get into their share of trouble.

Henry once threw a dart into a boy's leg and the boy jabbed him with a penknife in return.[7] He later recalled,

When a boy got in trouble he was brought up front and placed on the 'mourners bench' directly under the teacher's eye. You could get a good view of the stove from that location, and I sat there so much of the time that it was indelibly impressed on my memory.[8]

When Henry was ten, he transferred to the Miller School. His sister Margaret said it was because the teacher, Frank Ward, was changing schools.[9] Ward had taught Henry to do math in his head, and he wanted to continue studying with him.

Henry got into trouble at the Miller School, too. He was the leader of a group of rambunctious boys. Margaret recalled, "He didn't do much. He only told them what to do, and they very willingly did it."[10] They built a water wheel next to the schoolhouse, then dammed up a ditch to get enough water to run it. The wheel was hooked up to an old coffee mill, and they used it to grind potatoes, clay, and gravel.

Another time Henry and his friends built a "steam turbine" against the school fence. It exploded and caught the fence on fire. Henry later wrote, "Blew a piece through my lip, and a piece hit Robert Black in the stomach—abdomen, and put him *out*."[11]

The children carried their lunches to school, and one day Henry traded a beef sandwich for a piece of cake with frosting. "I thought I was making a good trade," he said.[12] His mother wondered why he was

sick, until little brother John told her, "He trades his sandwiches for cake."[13] She put a stop to that.

Henry really disliked farm work. His father got up at 6:00 A.M. to do the chores, but Henry was allowed to sleep. "The rest got up and went about their duties," Margaret later said, "and he stayed in bed."[14]

Henry's happy childhood came to an end in March 1876, when he was twelve years old. His mother died of complications after childbirth, and the baby also died. Henry said he felt as if "a great wrong had been done to me."[15]

William Ford's sister, Rebecca Flaherty, helped with the children for a while, then her daughter, Jane, took over. Henry's sister Margaret was only nine, but in a few years she took over the running of the house. She said, "She [Jane] was like a sister to us, not like a taskmaster."[16]

A couple of months after his mother's death, Henry was riding to Detroit in a farm wagon with his dad. Coming toward them, he saw a steam engine propelled by its own power. He later wrote,

> I had seen plenty of these engines hauled around by horses, but this one had a chain that made a connection between the engine and the rear wheels of the wagon-like frame on which the boiler was mounted . . . I was off the wagon and talking to the engineer before my father, who was driving, knew what I was up to.[17]

The engineer, Fred Reden, told Henry all about it. "Mr. Reden let me fire and run the engine many times that and the next year. He was a good and kind man."[18] When Henry realized that an engine could be used as a self-propelled vehicle, this was the moment he decided he was "by instinct an engineer."[19]

That same summer, Henry received his first watch for his birthday. He immediately took it apart and put it back together. Margaret recalled that when they got mechanical toys for Christmas, someone always said, "Don't let Henry see them! He'll take them apart!"[20]

Henry repaired a watch for a boy at Sunday school, then went on to fix many other clocks and watches for friends and neighbors. He made tweezers from a corset stay and screwdrivers from nails.

He said his father told him not to fix clocks unless he got paid. Later Ford said,

> I couldn't quit, so I used to go to my room at nine o'clock at night and wait until I thought my father had gone to sleep. Then I used to creep out of the house, go to the barn, saddle a horse, and ride away— sometimes many miles—to a place where I knew there was a watch or clock to repair. Many a time I did not get home until three o'clock in the morning.[21]

Margaret did not believe that. She said, "Father never forbade him to repair neighbors' watches. I never knew of him going out at night to get watches and bringing them back to repair them . . . I know

that Father never told Henry he should charge for the work he did."[22] It seems unlikely people would want him fixing watches at 3:00 A.M.

Henry always said that his mother thought he was a born mechanic. He insisted his father had no sympathy with his fascination with machines. Again, Margaret disagreed. "Father was quick to recognise [sic] Henry's ability in making new things. He was very understanding of Henry's demands for new tools in the shop, and ours was one of the best equipped in the neighborhood."[23]

During his teenage years, Henry went to church with his friend Edsel on Sunday nights, rode horses, ice skated in winter, and took long walks through the woods and along the Rouge River. However, he was just biding his time till he was old enough to go to Detroit and work in a machine shop. He finished school in 1879, at the age of sixteen, and decided the time had come.

3

INDEPENDENCE
AND
MARRIAGE

Henry Ford told people he left home without anyone knowing he was going, and that he had to walk the streets of Detroit, looking for work and a place to stay. "I was all but given up for lost," he said.[1] Most likely his father found him a job at Flower Brothers' Machine Shop. Years later, Ford denied he had ever worked there, although he eventually admitted it.

Frederick Strauss, who worked with him, remembered it this way:

> One morning I brought some valves into the office and while I was there I saw Henry Ford's father, and Henry was with him. I didn't know who they were, but the next day Henry came to work. . . . They put

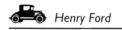

Henry Ford's inventiveness came out during his teenage years.

Henry in with me, and he and I got chummy right away. . . .[2] Apparently Henry's father knew the Flowers and came in and talked to them about Henry working in the shop.[3]

Henry Ford liked to think he was forced to sneak off to Detroit because of conflict with his dad. However, Margaret said, "I don't think there was any dispute at all. He just gradually led up to the move he took . . . We knew that at some time Henry would go to Detroit."[4]

A room was waiting for him at the home of his Aunt Rebecca Flaherty, William's sister. He later moved into a boardinghouse on Baker Street.

While working at Flower Brothers, Henry Ford also repaired watches for Robert McGill's jewelry shop. McGill had been a neighbor in Dearborn Township and offered to pay the boy fifty cents an evening. Henry worked at a workbench in the back, where no one would see him. McGill was afraid people would be upset to see a boy repairing their expensive watches.

Ford worked about nine months for the Flower Brothers, who ran one of the best machine shops in Detroit. An apprentice usually served four years, in order to learn a trade, but Henry Ford was impatient to move on and learn more. After he had learned to make valves and read blueprints, he got a job at Detroit Drydock Company, the largest shipbuilder in Detroit.

There he learned every phase of the machinist's trade. He enjoyed working with motors, and considered this the place where he got his training as a machinist. During his lunch break, he read engineering magazines. In *English Mechanic and World of Science*, he read of an internal combustion gas engine developed in Germany by Dr. Nicolaus Otto. Ford never forgot that article and from then on, he was obsessed with making a gas engine.

In 1882, when he was nineteen, Henry Ford moved back to the farm in Dearborn. His father had given him some land, and he wanted to clear it. A neighbor, John Gleason, was having trouble with a Westinghouse portable steam engine he had bought to saw wood and do threshing on his farm. This was the same sort of engine that had fascinated Ford when he was thirteen. Gleason paid Ford three dollars a day to work for him, so Ford spent the summer traveling from farm to farm, operating the machine. That fall, the Westinghouse company hired him to demonstrate their machines and service their engines on farms all over southern Michigan.

Ford's life in Dearborn was not all work, though. He learned to dance and attended social events around the area. On New Year's Eve 1885, he went to a dance given by the Greenfield Dancing Club. He was fascinated by a small, dark-eyed girl with chestnut hair. She was Clara Jane Bryant, the eighteen-year-old daughter of a nearby farmer.

Clara later said, "He made no impression on me at the time, and I didn't see him again for a year."[5] The second time they met, she was impressed with him. She went home and told her parents, "He's different. He doesn't just chatter about the music or talk about people. He's a serious-minded person."[6]

Meanwhile, Ford told Margaret he had realized after thirty seconds of conversation that Clara was the girl for him.[7] He began to court her in earnest, buying a green cutter (sleigh) so he could take her about in the winter. Besides sleigh rides, they enjoyed ice-skating and dancing. She showed great interest and confidence in his mechanical ideas, earning her the nickname "The Believer" from him.

Henry Ford and Clara Bryant were engaged on April 19, 1886. Ford cleared the land his father had given him, sawing the wood into lumber at his sawmill.

On April 11, 1888, the couple was married at the home of Clara's parents. They lived in a small

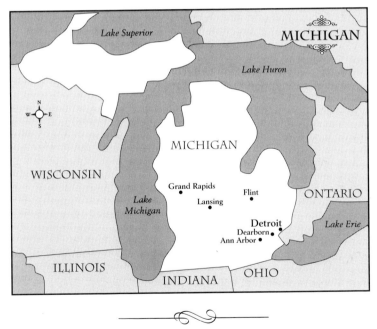

In 1891, Henry Ford and his wife moved from Dearborn, Michigan, to Detroit, so he could learn more about electricity and pursue his dream of building a horseless carriage.

house on the property while Henry built a new house with the lumber from his sawmill. Called the Square House, it was a story and a half high, with a workshop attached.

In late summer 1891, Ford told his wife he wanted to build a horseless carriage. He sketched out his idea on the back of a piece of her sheet music. She was enthusiastic. She was not so happy when he said they would need to move to Detroit so he could learn more about electricity. In Detroit, he got a job at the Edison Illuminating Company.

Even though Clara loved her house and life on the farm, she never complained. On September 25, 1891, they piled their furniture into a hay wagon and set off for Detroit.

4

RACE CARS AND BUSINESS FAILURES

Henry and Clara Ford moved into a little house a few blocks from the Edison Illuminating Company, where he worked nights. He started at $45 a month, but was soon making $75. Edison provided electrical power for 1,200 of the 1,650 Detroit residents who had electricity.

Ford set up a workshop at the plant so he could develop a gasoline engine in his spare time. In 1892, he taught a metalworking class at the YMCA. He made $2.50 a night and was allowed to use the shop for his own work.

Early in 1893, the Fords discovered they were expecting a baby. Clara never complained about the

time Ford spent on his experimenting, or the money he spent on materials. She believed in him and his ideas. Ford himself said, "I am always certain of results. They always come if you work hard enough. But it was a very great thing to have my wife even more confident than I was. She has always been that way."[1]

On November 6, 1893, Dr. William McDonald arrived at the Ford house on his bicycle, his medical bag strapped to the handlebars. He delivered a baby boy. Ford named him Edsel, for his old friend Edsel Ruddiman. The baby's middle name was Bryant, Clara's maiden name.

The week after Edsel was born, his father was promoted to chief engineer at Edison, and his salary nearly doubled. The family moved to a two-family house at 58 Bagley Avenue. It was only a five-minute walk from the plant. In his new job, Ford was on call twenty-four hours a day. He slept with his clothing laid out like a fireman and his boots ready to jump into at a moment's notice.

Behind the house was a brick shed, which the Fords shared with Felix Julien, a retired man who lived in the other side of the house. The shed held coal and wood that both families used as fuel. Ford moved his share inside the house to make room to experiment with engines in the shed. Julien got interested and he, too, moved his fuel inside.

On Christmas Eve 1893, Clara was working at the sink, getting the turkey ready for Christmas dinner. Ford brought in the engine he had built and asked her to help him test it. He connected a wire from the spark plug to the kitchen light and asked her to pour gasoline from a can into the intake valve, while he spun the flywheel. The engine coughed and sputtered, then roared into action, shaking the sink with its vibrations, while flames shot from the exhaust. Now that he knew the engine would work, he was ready to work on a horseless carriage.

Ford often worked late into the night in his makeshift shop. Jim Bishop and Edward Huff, friends from the Edison plant, frequently helped him. When Edsel was asleep, Clara often sat with her husband and kept him company as he worked.

Henry Ford was not the only one working on a horseless carriage, nor was he the first to build one. Throughout the United States and in several other countries, men were building automobiles. Brothers Frank and Charles Duryea built the first American gasoline car in Springfield, Massachusetts, in September 1893. Other Americans working on cars were Ransom E. Olds and Alexander Winton.

Jean Lenoir, a Belgian, had patented the first successful gasoline engine in Paris in 1860. Nicholas Otto and Eugene Langen, both Germans, had designed a more economical engine and displayed it

at the exhibit William Ford had attended in Philadelphia in 1876. Also in Germany, Gottlieb Daimler and Karl Benz built a gas-powered vehicle in 1886 and started manufacturing it in 1892.

By 1895, there were a few horseless carriages actually in operation in the United States. Charles King was the first in Detroit to test a gas-propelled vehicle on the city streets. He and Henry Ford were friends, and Ford accompanied him on his trial run on March 6, 1896. He rode a bicycle behind King as he drove his vehicle through the dark streets. The Detroit *Free Press* reported, "It was a most unique machine."[2]

Henry Ford wanted his car to be rugged, light-weight, dependable, and simple in design. After he had tested the Quadricycle on June 4, 1896, he began making changes to it. He hired a blacksmith from the Edison plant to help make an iron chassis. The new frame was strong enough to support more than one person, so he replaced the bicycle saddle with a carriage seat.

Henry Ford drove around the streets of Detroit, chaining the car to a lamppost so no one could steal it. People sometimes called him Crazy Henry and cursed at or threatened him for scaring their horses. Detroit Mayor William Maybury, an old family friend, gave him permission to drive on the streets.

Bringing the Family Along

Henry's first long automobile trip was to the family farm in Dearborn. Clara rode with him, holding Edsel on her lap. The wheels were closer together than those of a wagon, which meant that if one set of wheels was in a wagon rut, the other was up higher, causing the auto to tilt to one side. William Ford was interested, but refused to take a ride. "I can't see why I should risk my life just to get the thrill of riding in a carriage without a horse," he said.[3] Margaret was braver and went for a spin. She was bewildered by the speed at which it moved.

Henry said that gave him the "distinction of being the only licensed chauffeur in America."[4]

In August 1896, Ford and his boss, Alex Dow, attended a convention of illuminating companies in New York. Ford was thrilled to meet Thomas A. Edison, who was duly impressed when someone told him about the gasoline car. By that time, Edison was famous for inventing the phonograph, the electric light, and the motion picture. Ford drew him a diagram on the back of a menu and explained how the car worked, and Edison slapped him on the back. "Young man," he said, "you have the right idea. Keep right at it." To Dow he said, "This car has an advantage over the electric car because it supplies its own power."[5]

Ford sold his first Quadricycle for $200 and immediately began work on another one.

As he worked on the second car, Ford began to think about manufacturing automobiles to sell. The Duryea brothers were the only ones producing cars for sale at the time, although Ransom Olds and Alexander Winton were getting ready to do so.

By the summer of 1897, the Fords had moved to another home on East Alexandrine Avenue, and Edsel was entered in Miss Harriet Lodge's kindergarten.

Mayor Maybury gathered several backers and formed the Detroit Automobile Company on August 5, 1899. Henry Ford was chief engineer and a partner. They leased a large building on Cass Avenue, and Ford quit his job with Edison Illuminating Company. He tried without success to persuade some of his friends to join him in the endeavor.

Most of the parts were manufactured some-where else, and the men assembling the cars had little experience. Ford kept wanting to make changes, which caused delays. The first car was finally ready January 12, 1900. Instead of a passen-ger car, it was a delivery wagon, designed for delivering mail. It sold for $1,000.

A reporter from the Detroit *News-Tribune* took a ride in it with Ford. His headline the next day read:

SWIFTER THAN A RACE-HORSE IT FLEW OVER
THE ICY STREETS

Thrilling Trip on the First Detroit-Made Automobile, When Mercury Hovered About Zero.[6]

William Pring, a mechanic for the company, said he only saw three cars.[7] Ford insisted they made nineteen or twenty.[8] At any rate, the backers were unhappy with the production and dissolved the company in January 1901.

Ford was unhappy selling a car that was not the best he could make, and the investors did not want to wait forever. Ford said the directors were exploiting him. "The main idea seemed to be to get the money."[9] In fact, the company lost $86,000 in its fifteen months of existence.

Now Henry Ford turned his attention to building a racing car. To save money, he and his family moved in with his father and sister Jane who had moved into town. At a time when fathers were supposed to be remote authority figures, Ford enjoyed playing with Edsel. He loved to photograph him and Clara. Edsel was a quiet, sweet boy, who kept those qualities throughout his life. He had Clara's dark hair and eyes, but otherwise he looked like his father. Ford still worked many hours each day on his race car.

That first race car was finished in time for the first big automobile race in Detroit. Held at Grosse Pointe, Michigan, on October 10, 1901, the race

attracted much attention. The first event was for steam cars, and the second for electric cars.

Finally the race for gasoline cars was run. Originally set for twenty-five miles, it was shortened to ten miles, because the earlier races had taken so long. Three competitors were entered in the race, W. N. Murray of Pittsburgh, Alexander Winton from Cleveland, and a previously unknown mechanic, Henry Ford from Detroit. Murray withdrew when he discovered a leaking cylinder.

Winton, who had racing experience, led for the first three miles. Ford started to get the hang of turning corners and began to close the gap. When Winton's car started smoking, Ford pulled ahead and crossed the finish line in first place.

Ford was the talk of Detroit, but vowed he would never drive in a race again. "Boy, I'll never do that again," he muttered, as he got out of the racer. "I was scared to death."[10] He won $1,000 and a cut-glass punch bowl.

On November 30, 1901, the Henry Ford Company was formed, with five investors. Ford was supposed to come up with a small car to be produced for the public. However, he was more interested in working on a race car. About four months later, the company gave Henry Ford $900 and ended its association with him. Ford continued working on the race car.

His friend Ed "Spider" Huff was helping him with the car, as was C. Harold Wills, a young draftsman who drew up plans. Tom Cooper, the champion American racing cyclist, had saved $100,000 and paid for Ford to build two race cars.

The Arrow was red, and the 999, named after a fast New York City train, was yellow. The cars were ten feet long and had four huge cylinders on top of the engines. Henry said, "Their roar was enough to half kill a man."[11] The motor, instead of being under the seat as it had been in Ford's other cars, was between the front wheels.

Neither Ford nor Cooper wanted to risk his life driving either of the cars, so they got Barney Oldfield, another bicycle racer. Oldfield had never driven a car, but was a daredevil type. Spider Huff taught him to drive at Grosse Pointe, where the 999 had been towed in preparation for a race on October 25, 1902.

Ford had second thoughts and told Oldfield he should withdraw because he was risking his life. Oldfield replied, "Well, this chariot may kill me, but they'll say I was going like hell when she took me over the bank."[12]

Oldfield won the race. He covered the five miles in five minutes, twenty-eight seconds. A few weeks later he set the world's record for a mile in one minute, one second. The race brought Ford's name

to the forefront. He knew the time was right to start manufacturing cars. The publicity had made people aware that he could build a good car.

Alexander Malcomson, a leading coal merchant, and his lawyer suggested to Ford that they form a company to manufacture passenger cars. Henry would design the cars. Malcomson worked hard getting investors, and the Ford Motor Company was finally incorporated on June 16, 1903. John Gray

Barney Oldfield (left) drove Henry Ford's race car 999 to victory on October 25, 1902. The race helped get the attention of the media. Henry Ford stands to the right of Oldfield.

was president, Ford served as vice-president, and James Couzens, Malcomson's bookkeeper, was named secretary and business manager. Ford received a salary of $3,600 a year. Malcomson and Ford split 51 percent of the stock, and the investors got the other 49 percent. Henry Ford was finally in business.

5

FORD PIONEERS THE ASSEMBLY LINE

U nlike Henry Ford's first two business ventures, the Ford Motor Company was a success almost from the start. The young company could not afford to build a factory, so Ford rented a little wagon shop on Mack Avenue in Detroit to use as an assembly plant. There was not room to manufacture parts, so they subcontracted with other companies to do that. The Dodge brothers agreed to manufacture the engines.

The company hired ten workmen to assemble cars and paid an average rate of $1.50 a day for ten hours of work. Their goal was an output of fifteen cars a day.

The first car manufactured by Ford Motor Company was the Model A. It had a two-cylinder, eight-horsepower engine and was light and efficient. It had two speeds forward and one in reverse and could go up to thirty miles per hour. Henry Ford had designed the car, with the help of Harold Wills, who had worked with him on the racing cars.

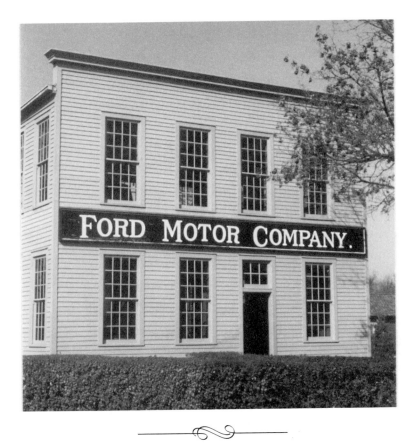

This is a reproduction of the first Ford Motor Company plant. The original building was formerly a wagon shop and was located on Mack Avenue in Detroit.

A Good Review for the Model A

An ad in *Motor World* in late 1903 said,

> *The most reliable machine in the world. A two-cylinder car of ample power for the steepest hills and the muddiest roads, built to stand the severest strains. The same genius who conceived the world's record maker—the 999—has made possible the production of a thoroughly practical car at a moderate price.* [1]

Ford was a couple of weeks short of forty years old when the Ford Motor Company made its first sale on July 15, 1903. Dr. E. Pfennig, a Chicago dentist, paid $850 for the first Model A. By the end of the year, Ford Motor Company had paid more than $100,000 in dividends to the stockholders. They sold seventeen hundred cars in the first fifteen months.

Henry Ford decided to race again and try to break the world's speed record for one mile. The race was set for January 12, 1904. A cindered path was laid out on the ice of Lake St. Clair, just northeast of Detroit.

Ed "Spider" Huff lay on the running board and blew into the tank to keep the gasoline feeding. Ford did set a world's record—39.4 seconds for a mile—but he never forgot the terror of that race.

"The ice seemed smooth enough . . . but instead of being smooth, the ice was seamed with fissures which I knew were going to mean trouble the moment I got up speed," he recalled. "At every fissure the car leaped into the air. I never knew how it was coming down. When I wasn't in the air, I was skidding, but somehow I stayed top side up and on the course."[2]

His race car had the same four-cylinder engine used in the new Model B. The publicity from the

Though the Model A was the first type of car produced by the Ford Motor Company, it was manufactured for decades. Pictured is a 1928 Model A Ford.

race helped car sales, which surpassed all expectations. The company paid a healthy dividend to its investors and still had money to build a new factory, a three-story building on Piquette Avenue. Since the parts were made elsewhere, they did not build a foundry to cast metal parts.

That same year Ford hired Charles Sorensen, a Danish immigrant, to help with the 999. In 1904, Ford named him boss of the pattern shop, where plans were drawn up for cars. He became one of Ford's most trusted assistants.

The only cloud on the horizon was a lawsuit filed against the Ford Motor Company by the Association of Licensed Automobile Manufacturers (ALAM). This group of companies was authorized by George Selden to build automobiles. He had patented a gasoline engine he had designed, and he insisted all manufacturers of cars with gasoline engines should pay him a fee.

Ford and Couzens stubbornly denied that Selden's invention had contributed anything to the automotive industry, so they decided to fight it. Ford had once applied for a license from ALAM and been turned down.

Ford and Couzens met with representatives of ALAM, who said they were prepared to go the limit to enforce Selden's claim. "Selden can take his patent and go to hell with it," roared Couzens.[3]

Ford, sitting with his chair tilted against the wall, feet dangling, shouted, "Couzens has answered you."[4] Fred Smith, ALAM president, told them that ALAM would put them out of business. Jumping to his feet, Ford pointed at Smith and yelled, "Let them try it!"[5]

Ford's lawyer, Ralzemond Parker, published an open letter in *Cycle and Automobile Trade Journal*, *Motor Age*, and *Horseless Age*. He stated that Ford Motor Company would continue to manufacture and sell gasoline cars. They considered Selden's patent without foundation in fact, and would not respect his claim.[6]

The suit was in court for several years. Meanwhile, in 1905, Ford Motor Company moved into its new Piquette Avenue plant, which was ten times as big as the old one. The company had now sold more than five thousand cars in a single season.

During its first five years of business, Ford Motor Company had tried out eight different models. In 1905–1906, their cheapest car was $1,000. Ford decided if they lowered the price, they would sell a lot more cars. They tried it the next year, and made a quarter of a million dollars, but Ford still was not satisfied with the product they were marketing.

Ford's father, William, who had been living with them, died on March 8, 1905, and the family moved closer to the plant. Ford bought Edsel a bike so he

could ride to school. Edsel always stopped at the plant on the way home. He stamped letters and helped out in other ways. Ford was pleased that Edsel was interested in the business. "I've got a boy I can be proud of," he said.[7] Edsel was a good student and loved to draw.

In 1905, Henry Ford decided it would be cheaper to make his own engines and car parts. He and Couzens incorporated the Ford Manufacturing

Henry Ford and his son Edsel were very close. Here father and son sit in the Ford Model F.

Company in November 1905 for this purpose. Malcomson, who had helped start Ford Motor Company, was furious at not being included, and resigned from the board to start his own company. Ford paid him $175,000 for his shares.

In 1906, John Gray died and Ford became president of the company. He also bought Gray's stock, and that of other stockholders. Now he and Couzens controlled the company.

The next year, Ford Motor Company and Ford Manufacturing merged, giving them the biggest industry under one roof in the state of Michigan.

Ford was still trying to design a car that pleased him. It had to be light in weight, rugged, easy to maintain, and dependable. His company should be able to produce it efficiently and sell it for a much lower price. He wanted every farmer and working man to be able to afford a car.

Ford talked about the coming car at the Detroit Automobile Show in 1907, saying, "It will be like forked lightning."[8]

He designed the car, the Model T, with the help of Joseph Galamb, a young Hungarian engineer who had worked in German automobile plants before coming to the United States. Vanadium steel, the lightest and strongest form of steel, made the new design possible. It could stand up under shocks that would crack regular steel.

"Mr. Ford first sketched out on the blackboard his idea of the design he wanted," Galamb said later.[9] Then Galamb made up a blueprint, and a mock-up was built. "Mr. Ford . . . was there practically all the time. There was a rocking chair [his mother's] in the room in which he used to sit for hours and hours at a time, discussing and following out the development of the design."[10]

Ford decided it would be most efficient to produce only one type of car, and the cars would all be alike. Even the color would be the same. Ford was fond of saying that you could get the Model T in any color you liked, "as long as it was black."[11] Other companies did not think he could stay in business with one type of car, and many of his associates agreed.

When the original Model T went on sale in October 1908, it sold for $850. The new automobile found immediate favor with the public. It was a simple car. Most men could do their own repairs with baling wire and cheap bolts. It stood up well on the bumpy, rutted back roads of the country at that time.

Orders flooded in, and by the end of September 1909, more than ten thousand Model T's had been sold. The Model T found instant popularity and was given many affectionate nicknames. At times it was called the "Flivver," "Leaping Lena," "Bouncing Betty," or "Galloping Snail." But the most widespread nickname was "Tin Lizzie." Stories and jokes

The Model T was Henry Ford's most popular car. Pictured is a 1914 Model T Ford.

about the cars abounded. Henry Ford thought they were great publicity. "A story on the front page is more valuable than advertising," he said.[12]

In 1909, the Fords finally built a home of their own on the corner of Edison and Second Avenue. The stone-trimmed brick house cost $293,253, including the landscaping Clara Ford ordered. Downstairs were a living room, dining room, kitchen,

library, butler's pantry, and servants' quarters. Upstairs were three bedrooms and tiled bathrooms.

Edsel returned to private school, enrolling in the Detroit University School. At fifteen, he had his first car, a Model N. This was a four-cylinder, moderately priced car designed to eliminate the faults of the Models C and F. Employees at the Ford plant said Edsel and his father were extraordinarily close. One clerk called them "twins in knowledge."[13]

Also in September 1909, Judge Charles Merrill Hough ruled that all automobile manufacturers were infringing on Selden's patent. Ford appealed. "We will fight to the finish," he said.[14] He insisted he would take it to the Supreme Court if he had to.

ALAM immediately ran ads threatening to prosecute anyone who bought a Ford car. "Don't buy a lawsuit with your car," they said.[15] Ford Motor Company retaliated with ads saying, "We will protect you against any prosecution for alleged infringements of patents."[16]

On January 9, 1911, three judges announced their verdict, saying that the defendants "neither legally nor morally owe him [Selden] anything."[17] As Ford was leaving New York, a reporter asked for a statement. He replied, "Whatever I'd say now might sound like boasting. I think the decision speaks for itself."[18]

On January 1, 1910, the Ford Motor Company had moved to its new plant in Highland Park. Ford had always tried to simplify his methods of operation and had tried out a crude assembly line at the Piquette plant. The workers built a line about forty feet long from railroad ties and put a chassis on the rails, pulling it along with a rope. Each workman connected his specific part to the chassis as it moved past. The company found they could not keep up with their orders, so they had to speed up production.

They tried various methods, but none worked until the world's first moving auto assembly line started in the spring of 1913. Workers lined up side by side, and a motorized conveyor belt moved the chassis along, while each worker did one job. "The man who places a part does not fasten it," explained Henry Ford. "The man who puts in a bolt does not put on a nut; the man who puts on the nut does not tighten it."[19] Their average chassis assembly time was now only ninety-three minutes.

"Every piece of work in the shop moves," said Ford. "It may move on hooks, on overhead chains . . . it may travel on a moving platform, or it may go by gravity, but the point is that there is no lifting or trucking."[20]

With the moving assembly line, Ford was able to turn out twice as many cars without increasing the

number of employees. Ford had found the key to producing a good car at a low price.

In the earlier years, Ford walked around the factory, talking with his workers and calling them by name. There were now too many employees for him to know by name, and he had lost touch with the workers.

Their treatment was becoming increasingly harsh. They had to be absolutely silent so they could concentrate. They were not allowed to smoke. They

Henry Ford's creation of the assembly line sped up production and made the automobile affordable to the average working man. Here, Model T's sit on the assembly line at the Highland Park plant.

worked a ten-hour day and had fifteen minutes for lunch. Many of these rules were put in force by Sorensen, Ford's trusted right-hand man, with Ford's approval. As the company sold more cars, employees were driven to work faster and faster. "Ford was one of the worst shops for driving men," said William C. Klann, a former executive.[21]

The foreman could fire anyone for no reason. Men were not promoted on the basis of seniority. Ford would not permit the workers to join a union. The unions were the only way for workers to have any say in their working conditions. In the summer of 1913, the labor union tried to get into the Ford plant, passing out papers focusing on working conditions there. They spoke of "Henry Ford, the Speed-up King." The company had some of the union workers arrested and canceled outdoor lunch privileges.

For the previous few years, labor had been abundant in Detroit, but by 1910, Ford was having trouble getting workers because of poor working conditions. He paid twenty-five cents an hour for unskilled labor. Workers quit often, and many fights broke out, due to stress and unrest. Forty to 60 percent of the employees were quitting each month.

John R. Lee, head of employment, limited the power of the foremen. They no longer decided who got raises. Instead, Lee gave everyone a 13 percent

raise. Turnover (workers quitting) dropped off, but Ford still was not satisfied. He decided since the executives and the stockholders were making huge sums of money, the employees should also share in the bounty.

Ford held a directors' meeting on Sunday, January 3, 1914. He said the workers needed a share in the vast amount of money the company was making. All agreed they could afford to raise wages. Ford wrote figures on the blackboard, showing how much it would cost to raise wages to three dollars a day, then increments up to five dollars. Most of the directors were strongly opposed. They said the company could not double wages.

There was another meeting two days later. The minutes stated, "The plan was gone over at considerable length." Couzens enthusiastically explained the plan, and finally convinced the other directors.[22]

They held a press conference, and Couzens did most of the talking. He said that starting January 12, Ford Motor Company would pay every worker at least five dollars a day, and would reduce the workday to eight hours. They would run three shifts a day. Ford added he preferred to have twenty thousand "prosperous and contented" workers, rather than giving a few "slave-drivers" and "multi-millionaires" all the profit.[23] They also called for four thousand new employees.

The country was in a depression, a bad time for the economy, with falling prices and widespread unemployment. The announcement had great impact. People were divided in their opinions. Most thought Ford was genuinely concerned about his workers. However, the other employers in Detroit were furious and criticized Ford for not having consulted them.

The result was a huge rush of applicants from all over the country. Nineteen thousand showed up the next morning, milling around in the open lot outside the plant. By the next week, regular employees could not get through the crowd. Hiring proceeded slowly, and men stood in line for hours in the freezing temperatures with no food.

When plant officials tried to clear a path for the regular employees, tempers flared and a riot broke out. After two hours, the police broke it up by spraying the men with fire hoses. The temperature was close to zero, and their clothes froze immediately. Some threw bottles and stones at the police and smashed windows in the factory. The Detroit *Journal* headline read: "ICY FIRE-HOSE DELUGE STOPS TWELVE THOUSAND IN RIOTOUS PUSH FOR FORD'S JOBS."[24]

Ford said his motive in raising wages was purely business. He claimed it would give him the pick of the workers.[25] History proved him right. Within the next year, profits skyrocketed.

6

THE PEACE SHIP

By the next summer, World War I had begun. Gavrilo Princip assassinated Archduke Francis Ferdinand of Austria and his wife on June 28, 1914. Princip was linked to a Serbian terrorist group known as the Black Hand. The Archduke was the heir to the throne of Austria-Hungary, and a month later, Austria-Hungary declared war on Serbia. Germany, Turkey, and Bulgaria joined on the side of Austria. They were called the Central Powers. Russia, France, England, and Italy came to the aid of Serbia, and were called the Allies. The United States tried to stay neutral, while at the same time building up its armed forces to be prepared for war.

President Woodrow Wilson, a Democrat, hated war, so he did all he could to keep the country out of it. The United States sold goods to both sides, but since England controlled the seas at first, more was sold to the Allies.

Henry Ford, a pacifist (one who does not believe in fighting), spoke out often and loudly against war. In August 1915, he told reporter Theodore Delavigue of the Detroit *Free Press* he would give up his fortune to secure peace. Headlines read: "HENRY FORD TO PUSH WORLDWIDE CAMPAIGN FOR UNIVERSAL PEACE: WILL DONATE LIFE AND FORTUNE TO COMBAT SPIRIT OF MILITARISM NOW RAMPANT."[1]

Delavigue continued to quote Ford, who was against preparation for war. His statements became more controversial and caused problems between Ford and James Couzens, vice-president of the Ford Motor Company. Couzens was in charge of advertising and refused to use ads where Ford expressed his pacifist views. When Ford insisted on using the ads, Couzens resigned as vice-president, although he remained on the board.

Ford said, "I would rather burn down my factory than supply materials for war."[2] He was quoted in the *New York Times* as saying, "'Murderer' should be embroidered in red letters across the breast of every soldier."[3]

The Peace Ship was one of Henry Ford's most generous ideas, and one of the most misunderstood. Rosika Schwimmer, a Jewish journalist from Budapest, Hungary, heard of Ford's stand for peace. She was aggressive and had already alienated some members of the peace movement in America, including Jane Addams, a social worker in Chicago who later won a Nobel Peace Prize.

Madame Schwimmer was in Detroit for a lecture and was determined to meet Henry Ford. She had originated a plan for peace based on a Neutral Conference for Continuous Mediation. This meant the United States and other neutral nations were offering to continue mediating until they could resolve the problems causing the hostilities. Ford's secretary, Ernest Liebold, would not let Madame Schwimmer in to see Ford.

In response, she met with Ralph Yonker, a *Detroit Journal* reporter who was on good terms with Ford. Yonker convinced Ford he should talk to her. She also wanted him to talk to Louis Lochner, a leader of the American peace movement, so she telegraphed Lochner, telling him he had an appointment with Mr. Ford.

Lochner arrived and was told no interview was scheduled. Liebold had left on a trip, and the secretary in charge felt sorry for Lochner and said he could squeeze him in after Madame Schwimmer.

This secretary introduced Lochner to Ford, saying, "This man is a victim of circumstance."[4] That aroused Ford's sympathy, and he talked to him. Ford invited both Lochner and Madame Schwimmer to lunch with him the next day in Dearborn. The Fords were living in a small house on the grounds where their new home was being built.

Theodore Delavigue, now Ford's peace secretary, lunched with them. Ford left Madame Schwimmer to talk to Clara and took Lochner and

Clara Ford rides as a passenger in a car her husband's company built.

Delavigue on a tour of the factory. He asked Lochner his opinion of Madame Schwimmer's proposal. Lochner thought continuous neutral mediation would work.

Over lunch, they agreed to go to New York and meet with the rest of the group who had worked on the neutral conference idea. Lochner suggested Ford talk to President Wilson and see if he would fund the plan, or at least give it official support.

On November 21, 1915, Ford and Lochner met with Jane Addams, Madame Schwimmer, and others in New York. Lochner suggested sending a peace delegation to Europe on a special ship. Ford jumped at the idea, and that afternoon he chartered the *Oscar II*, of the Scandinavia-American line. The ship was to sail on December 4.

Now Ford's first priority was a meeting in Washington, D.C., with President Wilson. Ford's tremendous popularity with the American people made Wilson willing to listen to him. Lochner accompanied him. When they entered the president's office, Ford made himself comfortable in an armchair, swinging his leg back and forth over the arm. He immediately told the president a Model T joke he had made up. The president chuckled, and then recited a limerick in return. They were off to a friendly start, but the president could not be pinned down to supporting the mission.

"I am by no means saying that the plan for continuous neutral mediation is not the best one that has yet been offered," President Wilson said,

> But as the head of a neutral nation I must also preserve neutrality of judgment when dealing with various proposals regarding the war. Suppose I commit myself to your plan. Who knows? Tomorrow a better plan may be offered which I shall be prevented from adopting because I have already committed myself to yours.[5]

Ford replied,

> Tomorrow at ten in New York, representatives of every big newspaper will come to my apartment [rented for the occasion] for a story. I have today chartered a steamship. I offer it to you to send delegates to Europe. If you feel you can't act, I will. I will then tell the newspapermen that I shall take a shipful of American delegates to Europe.[6]

The president would not commit himself, so Ford and Lochner left. As soon as they were outside, Ford turned to Lochner and said, "He's a small man."[7]

The next morning, Ford held his press conference. He told reporters he was sending a ship of peace delegates to Europe. "A man should always try to do the greatest good to the greatest number, shouldn't he?"[8] he asked. "I want to crush militarism and stop wars for all time. I intend to get the boys out of the trenches by Christmas."[9]

The newspapers ridiculed the idea from the start. Headlines in the New York *Herald Tribune* read:

"GREAT WAR ENDS CHRISTMAS DAY: FORD TO STOP IT."[10]

The Detroit *Free Press* wrote, "Repeated questions disclosed not the slightest evidence that Mr. Ford has a definite plan as to what he is going to do when he gets to Europe."[11]

Meanwhile, Madame Schwimmer and Jane Addams decided who to invite on the Peace Ship. Most refused the invitations. Even Ford's closest friends, Thomas Edison, John Burroughs, John Wanamaker, and Luther Burbank turned him down.

Of the forty-eight state governors, only Governor Louis Hanna of North Dakota accepted. The presidents of all major universities were invited, but none went. Ford decided not to invite members of Congress. He said, "I want those fellows to stay right in Washington and fight preparedness. They are more necessary there than on our Peace Ship."[12]

Ford invited some college students, and twenty-five of them accepted. The big newspapers and magazines were invited to send correspondents, at Ford's expense. Fifty-five correspondents, cartoonists, feature writers, and photographers accepted.

William Jennings Bryan, a pacifist and Wilson's first secretary of state, could not sail on the Peace Ship, but said, "I have seen Mr. Ford and am in hearty sympathy with the effort he is making, and hope to join the party at The Hague [the capital of the Netherlands where the talks would take place]."[13]

Ex-president William Howard Taft did not join the expedition because it was an unofficial undertaking. He did not think it could succeed unless the government backed it.

Some were very negative in their evaluation of the project. Former president Theodore Roosevelt said the Peace Ship was the "most discreditable" exploit in history.[14] Arthur Vandenberg, a newspaper editor, called it a "loon ship."[15] And Senator Thomas of Colorado called the delegation "an aggregation of neurotics."[16]

Mrs. Ford later recalled this as the most miserable period of her marriage. She told her husband that Madame Schwimmer and the others "care not if [you] die, just so long as [you] go along to lend [your] name and provide money to be squandered."[17] Mrs. Ford, her spiritual advisor, Reverend Samuel Marquis, and Ford's chauffeur-bodyguard, Ray Dahlinger, spent most of the night trying to talk him out of going.

Ford refused to be swayed. He gave Edsel power of attorney and made out a will leaving everything to him. Marquis finally agreed to go along to watch over him for his wife.

The morning of December 4 was cold and rainy, but fifteen thousand people came to the dock at

Hoboken, New Jersey, to see the Peace Ship sail. Henry, Clara, and Edsel Ford arrived at the pier in a Model T.

A carnival-like atmosphere prevailed. One band played on board the ship, while another on the pier tried to outdo it. A man hired by Madame Schwimmer as social director yelled introductions through a megaphone as people came on board. Someone gave them two squirrels in a cage to take as mascots. A reporter named them "Henry F. Acorn" and "William H. Chestnut."[18]

Thomas Edison and his wife, Mina, came on board to see them off. Ford grabbed Edison's hand and said repeatedly, "You must stay on board and go with us." Sixty-eight-year-old Edison was largely deaf, so Ford finally yelled in his ear, "I'll give you a million dollars if you'll come."[19] Edison just smiled, not appearing to understand him. He and his wife went ashore just before the ship sailed.

At 3:25 P.M., the ship backed slowly from the pier, as the band played, "I Didn't Raise My Boy to Be a Soldier." Henry Ford leaned over the railing, throwing three dozen American Beauty roses to the crowd and waving his derby. Clara watched from the pier, crying. A man calling himself "Mr. Zero" dove into the icy waters, saying it was a "swim for peace." The crew fished him out.

Henry Ford and Thomas Edison, two well-known inventors, would remain friends throughout life.

During the two weeks at sea, the delegates got thoroughly tired of Rosika Schwimmer's aggressive ways. She carried a mysterious black handbag, saying it contained secret documents that indicated the readiness of some of the countries involved in the war to consider mediation. She insisted on being in charge of everything, and by the time they arrived in Norway, few passengers could tolerate her.

Ford, on the other hand, was popular with the passengers. He was accessible to those who wanted to talk, eating breakfast each morning with the students. Twice a day he met with the reporters. He won over many of them with his friendliness and down-to-earth attitude.

Lella Secor, a young journalist from the Seattle *Post-Intelligencer* described him as "one of the most unique and most delightful men I have ever met. He is simple, unassuming, witty, and a man of great ideals."[20]

Another newsman said, "I came to make fun of the whole trip, but my editor's going to have the surprise of his life. I tell you I believe in Henry Ford and I'm going to say so, even if I lose my job for it."[21]

Even the reporter from the *New York Times* agreed that all the newspapermen "have learned in these few days an immense respect and liking for the character and abilities of Henry Ford."[22]

Many reporters and cartoonists did send material to their papers ridiculing the Peace Ship. Someone suggested that Ford should refuse to send the stories over the wireless. He merely said, "The reporters are my guests. I wouldn't for the world censor them."[23]

Just before the ship passed Great Britain, Ford was walking on the deck one morning, when a huge wave washed over and drenched him. He became ill and had to stay in his stateroom the last few days of the voyage. Some correspondents reported to their papers that Ford was inaccessible because Lochner had tied him to his bed.[24]

Another group burst into his suite, saying "Mr. Ford, J. Pierpont Morgan [a well-known financier] was dead six hours before any newspaper knew about it. So we've come to see for ourselves whether you are still alive."[25]

It was twelve degrees below zero when the ship docked in Norway at 4:00 A.M. on December 18. Most delegates rode sleds to the hotel, but Henry Ford insisted on walking, then collapsed when he got there.

Marquis and Dahlinger were worried about him and put him to bed in a suite that could only be reached through their rooms. Finally he held a press conference in his room on December 22. The weak, sickly man in a nightshirt only wanted to talk about tractors.

Dr. Kuren of the Red Cross diagnosed Ford's illness as influenza and severe nervous exhaustion. He recommended a stay at a health resort. Marquis talked Ford into returning home, instead. "Guess I'd better go home to Mother," Ford told Lochner. "I told her I'd be back soon. You've got this thing started now and can get along without me."[26]

At 4:00 A.M. on Christmas Eve, Marquis, Dahlinger, and Ford tried to sneak out of the hotel so the group would not know Ford was leaving. But Madame Schwimmer had found out they were going, and a group of delegates were there, shouting insults at Marquis and accusing him of kidnapping Ford.

When they arrived back home after an uneventful crossing, a Coast Guard launch came to meet the ship as it docked in heavy fog. At the Waldorf Hotel, Ford talked to reporters. One asked, "Do you think the Peace Ship was worth what you put into it?"[27]

He answered immediately, "I do. A man is always repaid for what he spends when he gets results, and making people talk in this case spells results."[28]

The delegates who remained in Europe were quite well received in the Scandinavian countries, Holland, and Switzerland. They made The Hague their headquarters and issued an Easter "Appeal to the Belligerents," asking the fighting nations to negotiate peace. They finally had to end their campaign when the United States entered the war on April 7, 1917.

7

WAR, TRIALS, AND RETIREMENT

B y early 1916 when he returned from the Peace
Ship, Henry Ford had become a legend in the
United States. He had already been popular as the
man who made it possible for most people to own a
car. Now he had become even more famous through
his exploits with the Peace Ship.

In June, President Wilson called up the National
Guard to protect the United States's southern
border from raids by Mexican guerrillas. The
Chicago *Tribune* asked Ford's office if workers
who were mobilized by the National Guard would
receive their pay and be reinstated in their jobs
when they returned. Without checking with Ford,

Frank Klingensmith, Ford's personal secretary, told the reporter the men would neither be paid nor reinstated.[1]

Actually, Ford was paying them and giving them their jobs back when they returned. But the *Tribune* printed Klingensmith's statement with a headline "FLIVVER PATRIOTISM."[2] They ran an editorial the next day, accusing Henry Ford of being "not merely . . . an ignorant idealist, but . . . an anarchist [a person who believes in no government] enemy of the nation which protects him in his wealth."[3]

Ford ignored the editorial until his lawyer, Alfred Lucking, urged him to sue them for libel, which he did. It took a while for the case to come to trial.

Meanwhile, the Fords moved to a new house on the Rouge. They had decided to leave the Edison Avenue house to get away from the public. People were always at their door, asking for money, job interviews, or help with inventions. They had finally been forced to place a guard at the front door.

Ford bought some heavily wooded land along the Rouge River and had made it into a nature sanctuary. He put up hundreds of birdhouses and feeders and released deer. He had not planned to build a house there until Clara said, "If we could build the house we want, I'd like to build out in Dearborn."[4]

The house, which ended up costing over a million dollars, was built of Indiana limestone and had fifty-six rooms. In an effort to keep Edsel at home, Ford had included a swimming pool, bowling alley, and golf course. Clara had the grounds beautifully landscaped, with an artificial lake, several pools, and six types of gardens. They named it Fair Lane.

There was a guard at the gatehouse, and the entire property was fenced. "I like privacy in my home," Ford explained. "Without this protection, my place would become a public park overrun by strangers."[5]

Soon the Fords were in the spotlight for another reason—Edsel was getting married. This was the end of the Fords' hopes that the golf course and bowling alley would keep him with them at Fair Lane for many years.

Edsel, now twenty-three, had worked at the Ford plant since graduation from high school. He would have qualified for any college and he had expected to go, but Henry distrusted higher education, so Edsel was learning the business firsthand.[6]

In 1915, he became secretary of the company, with a seat on the board of directors. He was a quiet, modest man. He was popular with the workers, who called him "Mr. Edsel." He looked a lot like his father, and wore expensive suits and custom-made shoes.

Edsel was concerned about the workers. He was less stiff and more fun-loving than his father. He loved jokes and he could laugh at himself, as his father never could.

While the Fords lived on Edison Avenue, Edsel had met Eleanor Clay, who lived a few blocks away, at a dancing class. Eleanor's father had died in 1908, and her uncle, Joseph Hudson, had taken her and her mother and sister to live with him. The Hudsons were a prominent family and lived in a huge mansion.

Edsel and Eleanor shared a love of golf, popular music, yachting, and dancing. They had known each other for several years, and when she graduated from high school in June 1916, they announced their engagement.

The wedding was held in the Hudson mansion on November 1, 1916. Reporters were disappointed at the lack of pomp and ceremony. A reporter from the Detroit *Free Press* remarked, "I don't think I saw $1000 of jewels."[7]

John and Horace Dodge, who had made parts for Ford's first automobiles, attended the reception and seemed on friendly terms with the Fords. The Dodge brothers were now stockholders and had seats on the board of Ford Motor Company. The next day they filed a suit against the company. They wanted to halt work on the Rouge plant and to force the company to distribute 75 percent of the cash surplus as dividends. They thought Henry Ford was keeping too large a share of the profits for himself.

Meanwhile, the war in Europe dragged on and the United States became more involved. In February 1917, President Wilson severed diplomatic relations with Germany. Henry Ford stopped his antiwar statements. When the United States declared war in April, he said it was "the best thing that ever happened."[8]

Edsel Ford and Eleanor Clay married on November 1, 1916.

Other pacifists made similar turnabouts. William Jennings Bryan, who had been a passionate pacifist, now stated, "A declaration of war closes discussion."[9]

Ford promised he would operate his factories for the war effort without a cent of profit.[10] He received an order in May for two thousand Model T chassis (frames) to be used as ambulances. The Highland Park plant manufactured nearly a million steel helmets. They also built motors for aircraft.

The biggest project Ford undertook was building submarine patrol vessels. These were designed by the Navy and nicknamed Eagle boats. Ford needed a larger plant in which to build them, and the Rouge location was the logical place. The finished boats could sail to the Atlantic, via the Great Lakes and St. Lawrence River. Congress voted to supply the money to widen the river and construct the plant.

That spring, the first of the 112 Eagle boats the government had ordered was begun, and two months later the first one was launched into the Rouge River. The plant ran three production lines, each working on seven boats. Ships had never been produced on an assembly line before.

Ford employees coined a slogan: "An Eagle a Day Keeps the Kaiser [German leader] Away."[11] They were not quite that efficient, however. On November 17, 1918, an armistice was declared. This was a cease-fire preliminary to the peace treaty. By that time, only seven boats had been finished and delivered.

Ford blamed the designers, who kept changing the specifications. Also the engineers had a difficult time adapting their auto building techniques to ship-building.

Throughout this time, Edsel Ford had worked for Ford Motor Company, after being deferred from military service. He had stated, "I am perfectly willing to be drafted with the rest of the young men of this community."[12] His father was not willing, though, and insisted he apply for an exemption, which was granted due to his importance to the company.

The press was unmerciful in their condemnation of Edsel. Congressman Nicholas Longworth, son-in-law of former president Theodore Roosevelt, said that seven young men would go through the war unhurt—the six sons of the Kaiser and Edsel Ford.[13]

As the war drew to a close, President Wilson asked Henry Ford to run for the Senate. Wilson wanted his plans for a League of Nations included in a peace treaty. The League would be a peacekeeping organization of world powers, similar to the United Nations today. In order for the peace treaty to be ratified with this clause, he needed one more Democratic vote.[14]

Michigan was a Republican state. "You are the only man in Michigan who could be elected on the Democratic ticket," Wilson told him. "So I want you to run for the Senate. You can help bring about the peace we both so much desire."[15]

Ford was reluctant, but Wilson insisted. "Mr. Ford," he said, "we are living in very difficult times—times when men must sacrifice themselves for their country."[16] Ford finally agreed to run against Republican Truman Newberry.

Newberry had served as secretary of the Navy in Theodore Roosevelt's cabinet and was in favor of war. He spent large amounts of money campaigning all over the state. He also made much of Edsel's deferment.

Henry Ford made no speeches and spent no money. However, he was popular enough among the people that he had a chance to win.

Two days before the election, the Republicans ran a large ad in the Detroit *Free Press* calling Ford a "Hunlover." (Hun was a derogatory term for German.) It said,

> Carl Emde, a German alien and sympathizer, is boss of the drafting work on the Liberty Motor at the Ford plant . . . If Carl Emde wishes to make plans and photographs of the Ford plant of Liberty Motor for use by the enemies of the U.S., Henry Ford is willing to give him the chance to do it.[17]

Emde was actually a United States citizen and completely loyal to the United States.

Ford insisted on contacting Emde personally before putting a rebuttal in the papers, and the statement missed getting in the state edition of the paper. It only appeared in the Detroit editions, so thousands of voters never saw it.

This probably cost Ford the election, since he easily carried Detroit, but lost in a close race in other parts of the state. He lost by fewer than

Henry Ford's friends were often as well known as he was. Here he sits with Thomas Edison (center) and Harvey Firestone (right).

twenty-two hundred votes. This gave the Republicans forty-nine seats and the Democrats forty-seven and may have been a factor in the defeat of Wilson's proposal for a League of Nations. Although the United States did not join, the League of Nations was created.

A month and a half later, at the age of fifty-five, Henry Ford resigned as president of the Ford Motor Company. Edsel succeeded him.

In February, the supreme court of Michigan ruled in the Dodge brothers' suit. The Ford Motor Company must pay the stockholders a little over $19 million from their surplus profits, plus 5 percent interest since the date the suit was filed. It ruled that a business corporation was run primarily for the profit of its stockholders, so most of the profit must go to them. However, it ruled that the court must not interfere with the company's expansion, so the building of the Rouge plant went on.

A month later, the Los Angeles *Examiner* ran the following headline: "HENRY FORD ORGANIZING HUGE NEW COMPANY TO BUILD BETTER, CHEAPER CAR."[18] The new company would be in direct competition with Ford Motor Company. Stockholders and Ford dealers panicked.

Price of stock fell, which was what Henry Ford had expected. Then he sent secret agents to buy up the other stockholders' shares. Most were eager to sell, but James Couzens figured out what was going on and refused to sell at the lower price. Ford finally paid what Couzens asked.

When Henry Ford heard the news that all the stock belonged to the family, he "danced a jig all

Famous Men on Vacation

The rural excursions of Henry Ford and his famous friends provided regular summer features for American newspapers between the years 1918 and 1924. During the trial, Ford had taken a holiday with Thomas Edison, John Burroughs, and Harvey Firestone. The previous summer they had gone camping in the Adirondack Mountains of New York State, and had decided to make it an annual event. This time they went through upstate New York to New England. They took half a dozen cars and trucks, a Model T fitted out as a mobile kitchen, a kitchen tent with refrigerator, and a dining tent with a table that seated twenty. Each man had his own ten-by-ten tent, complete with wooden floor, electricity, folding cot, mattress, and bedding.

Burroughs wrote: "When we have settled on a camping site, Mr. Edison settles down in his car and reads or meditates; Mr. Ford seizes an axe and swings it vigorously till there is enough wood for the campfire . . . He is also a vigorous walker, and from every camp, both morning and evening, he sallied forth for a brisk half-hour walk. His cheerfulness and adaptability on all occasions, and his optimism in regard to all the great questions, are remarkable."[19]

around the room."[20] Now he owned 55 percent of the stock, while Edsel owned 42 percent and Clara 3 percent. "Of course," Edsel said, "there will be no need of a new company now."[21] The whole idea of a rival company had been just to incite panic and cause stockholders to sell him their stock at a lower price.

Ford's libel suit against the Chicago *Tribune* also came to trial in the summer of 1919. The trial had been moved to a neutral location, Mount Clemens, Michigan.

Unfortunately, Ford's attorney, Lucking, had based his suit on the whole editorial, rather than just the term "anarchist," which had been considered libelous in past cases. The opposition set out to prove that Henry Ford was, indeed, ignorant. Their lawyers cross-examined him on his knowledge of American history, which was sketchy to say the least. They made him appear ridiculous.

The jury did find the *Tribune* guilty of libel, ordering the paper to pay costs. Unfortunately for Ford, the costs were to be based on the difference between Henry Ford as the jurors saw him, and Henry Ford as portrayed in the editorial. They believed he was not an anarchist, but awarded him six cents, implying that they thought the part of the editorial accusing him of being ignorant was true.

8

GREENFIELD VILLAGE AND THE HENRY FORD MUSEUM

O n his way home from the *Tribune* trial in 1919, Henry Ford turned to his secretary, Ernest Liebold, and said,

> I'm going to start up a museum and give people a true picture of the development of the country. That's the only history that is worth observing, that you can preserve in itself. We're going to build a museum that's going to show industrial history, and it won't be bunk [nonsense]! We'll show the people what actually existed in years gone by and we'll show the actual development of American industry from the early days, from the earliest days that we can recollect up to the present day.[1]

From the beginning, Ford wanted two separate facilities. A village of early American life would have historic buildings and show how people had lived and worked. A museum would showcase man's technological and cultural progress.

In 1919, the house where Ford was born was threatened. A major road was to be built through the family's farm, and the house stood in the way. Ford decided to move the house and barns and to restore them to the way they were in 1876, the year his mother died.

The buildings were moved about two hundred feet east. Men dug through the area around the foundation. Ford was able to have his mother's china reproduced from broken pieces of dishes. One day they found a pair of rusty old skates. Fred Black, one of the workers, recalled: "Mr. Ford recognized these skates as his own when he was a boy. I remember his great delight. I don't think he could have been given anything in the world that would have pleased him quite as much as those old, rusty skates."[2]

Most of the restoration was completed by 1926, and the house became a "plaything for Mr. and Mrs. Ford," according to Edward J. Cutler, who supervised the project. "They'd have parties over there, and they'd get all dressed up. The men and women were in the old costumes, and they'd dance, and they'd have their orchestra over there."[3]

This was the beginning of Greenfield Village in Dearborn, Michigan. In 1923, Ford bought the little red Scotch Settlement schoolhouse where he had started his education. For several years he operated it as an experimental school for children ages three to six. Here they learned from McGuffey's first *Reader*, combined with new visual learning techniques.

Ford and his aides scoured farms and antique shops, looking for artifacts that would fit into the restoration. He stored excess items in the office of his tractor plant. When the public learned of his search, he was flooded with offers of antiques. When the company transferred tractor operations to the Rouge in 1920, the tractor plant was used to store the artifacts.

By 1923, Ford had amassed the largest collection of Americana (objects having to do with the United States and its history) in the world. He had collected both technological items and everyday items, such as home furnishings. All the items that were donated or bought had to be put into working order. Cutler, the supervisor, had an office in the building among the clutter of thousands of historical artifacts.

C. J. Smith restored cars. He noted, "All of those old cars were rebuilt better than new. We even had new tires made for them . . . Mr. Ford showed a lot of interest in this work; he was always around."[4]

Ford said in 1926, "One of these days the collection will have its own museum at Dearborn, and there we shall reproduce the life of the country in its every age."[5]

Ford had Cutler draw plans for a village. Cutler's early sketches were based on New England villages, where public buildings surrounded a village green.

Ford liked the plan, but made endless changes, sometimes after buildings were in place. The first building to arrive on the village site was an old country store from Waterford, Michigan. Ford agreed to build a new brick structure in Waterford, so the owner could continue his business.[6] Other buildings included the Luther Burbank Office, an old firehouse from New Hampshire, and the Wright Brothers' bicycle shop from Dayton, Ohio. Construction proceeded at a fever pitch.

In 1928, Ford decided to recreate Thomas Edison's Menlo Park Compound, and had six buildings moved—brick by brick—from New Jersey. This became one of the focal points of the village. Work on the restoration proceeded quickly, since Ford had decided to dedicate it on the fiftieth anniversary of Edison's invention of the lightbulb.

Also in 1928, Henry Ford hired architect Robert O. Derrick, a friend of Edsel's, to design the museum. Derrick suggested building it like Independence Hall, and Ford liked the idea.[7] Thomas Edison signed his name on the wet concrete cornerstone on September 27, 1928, and actual construction began on the museum the next April.

In September 1929, school began in the village. Ford enrolled thirty-two children from fourth through seventh grades, and they attended classes in the old Scotch Settlement School. Eventually the school system was expanded to include nine school buildings, and children from kindergarten through high school were educated there.

The entire front section of the museum, with Independence Hall in the center, was finished in time for the October 21, 1929, dedication. The mechanical arts hall at the back of the museum, which covered eight acres, took several more years to complete.

The day of the dedication, Mr. and Mrs. Thomas Edison arrived on a special train, accompanied by President and Mrs. Herbert Hoover and Clara Ford. They toured the muddy streets of the village in enclosed, horse-drawn carriages.

NBC broadcast a radio program honoring Edison at 7:30 P.M. A candlelit dinner was held inside the Independence Hall part of the museum. Henry Ford did not give a speech, but Edison and President Hoover did.

After dinner, Ford, Hoover, and Edison traveled to the semi-darkened Menlo Park Laboratory.

Edison and his former assistant, Francis Jehl, had built a lightbulb identical to the one they had made fifty years earlier.

Graham McNamee of NBC described the big moment like this:

> But here is Mr. Edison again. While he was at the power house, Mr. Jehl sealed up the old lamp, and it is now ready . . . Will it light? Will it burn? Or will it flicker and die, as so many previous lamps had died? Oh, you could hear a pin drop in this long room. Now the group is once more about the old vacuum pump. Mr. Edison has the two wires in his hands now; now he is reaching up to the old lamp; now he is making the connection. It lights![8]

Fittingly enough, the museum at that time was called the Edison Institute.

Since its opening, many exhibits have been added to both the museum and the village. It now covers ninety-three developed acres and is the nation's largest and most-visited indoor/outdoor museum, with over a million visitors every year.

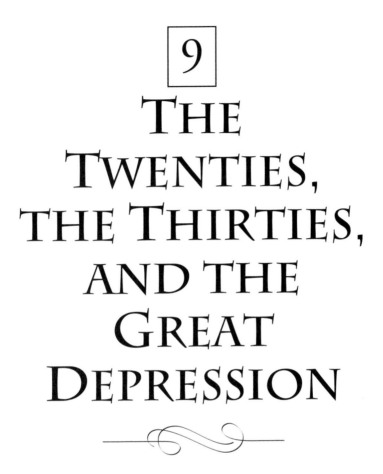

9

THE
TWENTIES,
THE THIRTIES,
AND THE
GREAT
DEPRESSION

Going into the 1920s, there was an atmosphere of turbulence in the United States. There were economic problems and violence was on the rise. There was a dramatic increase in unrest among laborers.

At this time, Henry Ford was one of the most popular men in the United States. However, an unpleasant part of Ford's character came to light in 1920.

He had started a newspaper, the *Dearborn Independent*, in January 1919 as a place to express his views. In May 1920, the paper began a series of articles attacking the Jews.

Somehow on the Peace Ship, Ford had become convinced that the war had been started by "the international Jew."[1] Some think his unpleasant experiences with Rosika Schwimmer, who was Jewish, caused his prejudice.

The articles described Jews as a menace and accused them of starting World War I. It said they were trying to control the commerce, finances, and governments of the world. Since the *Independent* had a limited circulation, Ford had the articles bound into books and sold throughout America and Europe.

The articles caused bitter resentment among Jews and many others. The series ended abruptly after ninety-one weeks. However, in 1924, the *Independent* attacked Aaron Sapiro, a prominent Jewish lawyer in Chicago. It accused Sapiro, who was helping to organize farm cooperatives, of attempting to defraud American farmers and control agriculture in the United States.

Sapiro filed a million-dollar libel suit against Ford, who claimed that the articles had not injured anyone. He said Herman Bernstein, editor of a Jewish newspaper, had told him on the Peace Ship that "the international Jews" had caused the war.[2] Bernstein denied making such a statement and filed a suit of his own.

A mistrial was declared when Sapiro's suit came to trial in Detroit in March 1927. Ford, finally convinced that the information in the articles could not be proven, issued a statement and an apology. The statement said that Henry Ford had no knowledge of what was being published. This is hard to justify, since he controlled the content of the paper. Bernstein also dropped his suit after the apology.

During this time, Ford was close to Edsel's four children. Henry II had been born in 1917, Benson in 1919, Josephine (known as Dodie) in 1923, and William in 1925. The children spent much time at Fair Lane, enjoying the swimming pool, hunting for birds' nests, and sleeping in the hayloft in the barn. Ford built them miniature autos, tractors, and farm tools. At Christmastime, he built a Santa Claus house on the estate and the grandchildren would bring their friends there to watch Santa getting the toys ready.

Meanwhile, the Ford Motor Company continued to manufacture only the Model T. Early in the 1920s, Edsel suggested diplomatically that it would be good to start making a more modern car. With the improvement in streets and roads, the Model T

The Ford family shared many good times at the Fair Lane Estate.

was no longer the only car that could stand up to the conditions.

More women were helping choose the family car, and they wanted something more appealing than the boxy black Model T. Chevrolet was bringing out a nicer-looking car at a comparable price.

Edsel was president of the company, but Henry Ford still ran the business. He stubbornly refused to make any changes until sales in 1926 dropped by a quarter of a million cars. Then he reluctantly agreed that maybe a change was necessary.

On May 25, 1927, he announced that no more Model T's would be made. The next day, the fifteen millionth Model T rolled off the assembly line. It had the number "15,000,000" painted in silver on the side.

People waited eagerly to see what the new Ford car would look like. Henry Ford did much of the engine design for the new car, while Edsel was in charge of the body. "We have a pretty good man in my son," Ford said, in a moment of rare praise. "He knows how a car ought to look, and he has mechanical horse sense, too."[3]

All automotive operations were moved from Highland Park to the Rouge, which was shut down for over six months for the changeover. The new Model A would require fifty-six hundred new parts, and machines had to be built to make them. Ford Motor Company hired hundreds of skilled tool and die makers (machinists who make and maintain machine parts) to work on them.

Walter Reuther was one of these men. He compared the two plants,

> These two places were as different as day and night. Highland Park was civilized, but the Rouge was a jungle. The humanitarianism Henry Ford had shown so dramatically in his early days just didn't exist any more. Sorensen and Pete Martin were in charge of production and that is all they cared about.[4]

People speculated about what the new car would be like. All kinds of rumors were repeated, but the secret was closely guarded. The new Model A's were covered with canvas bags when they were shipped to showrooms so no one could see them before December 2.

Ford launched a 1.3 million-dollar campaign in two thousand daily newspapers to introduce the new car. Almost four hundred thousand people had already ordered one, sight unseen.

On December 2, 1927, the Model A was unveiled. The New York *Herald Tribune* estimated that a million people flocked to Ford showrooms around the country to see the new car. There was already a crowd outside the Ford headquarters on Broadway at 3:00 A.M. The *New York World* reported, "Excitement could hardly have been greater had Pah-wah, the sacred white elephant of Burma, elected to sit for seven days on the flagpole of the Woolworth Building."[5]

As soon as the new auto was introduced, Ray Dahlinger drove one across the country and back. Dahlinger, who served Ford in many capacities, drove to Los Angeles, San Francisco, New York and back to Dearborn. He left on December 2 and arrived home December 23. This drive, through wintry conditions of ice, snow, mud, and sand, showed the durability of the new model. Dahlinger averaged 40.9 miles per hour and 20.1 miles to a gallon of gasoline.

The new car came in several colors and types. The biggest change was in the transmission, plus the hand crank was gone. It boasted hydraulic brakes and safety glass in the windshield, and would cost less than the current Chevrolet.

The Model A sold well for a while, but on October 29, 1929, the stock market crashed. It was the first visible sign of the Great Depression, although there had been some problems with the economy for several months. Banks failed and many people lost all their savings. By 1932, over a quarter of the nation's work force was unemployed. Things were not much better in rural areas. Many farmers lost their land. They could not sell their agricultural goods, since the city people did not have money to buy them.

The car business declined. Ford tried to help by cutting prices and expanding his plants. He also raised wages for a time, until he could no longer afford to do so. He created jobs, by building a two-mile-long tunnel connecting the Rouge plant with the Detroit River. In December 1931, Ford and Edsel agreed to install a new V-8 engine in their Model B car. This made their cars faster than their competitors' cars that had six-cylinder engines.

In 1932, Ford made only one-fifth as many cars as the company had made in 1929. Ford was forced to lay off people and cut wages. During the first three years of the Depression, Ford Motor Company lost $125 million. Since the company had made $900 million profit in the past, it was in no danger of bankruptcy.

Henry Ford helped people in many ways during the Depression. He set up a lab and hired Robert Boyer to try to find industrial uses for farm produce. He sent thousands of his unemployed plant workers to work on his farm projects.

He set up a new school to train recent high school graduates who could not find jobs to work in the factory. He did not believe in charity, as he

Getaway Cars

Gangsters used the Model B V-8 as a getaway car, since it would take off so fast. John Dillinger, a famous gangster, wrote Ford a letter saying, "Hello, Old Pal. You have a wonderful car. It's a treat to drive one."[6]

Clyde Barrow, who with Bonnie Parker terrorized the country, asserted, "I have drove Fords exclusively when I could get away with one."[7] When they were finally killed in a shoot-out, Bonnie and Clyde were in a V-8 Ford they had stolen. Police pumped 107 bullets into the car, but after their bodies were removed, the car could be driven away.

thought it was degrading to people. Instead of soup kitchens, he set up commissaries where people could buy food on IOU's. It was the first time he had ever done business on credit.

On March 7, 1932, the Communist party (a party based on the belief that society as a whole should own all means of production, distribution, and exchange of goods) staged what they called a "Hunger March." Three thousand men marched from downtown Detroit to the Rouge plant, waving red flags and making unreasonable demands. They wanted Ford to go to a six-hour day, get rid of all practices they considered unfair, give free medical care, and give employees the right to form a union. Most of the men on the march were not Communists, but unemployed men who were desperate. None of them had ever worked for Ford, and many had never worked at all.

The Dearborn and Detroit police tried to break up the mob with tear gas, but the wind blew it away. When they reached the gates of the plant, guards again got out the fire hoses and turned them on the crowd. They retaliated by throwing a barrage of objects.

Someone yelled, "We want Bennett."[8] Ford's tough personnel manager stepped out to talk to the men and was attacked. A rock hit him in the head and knocked him unconscious. Police opened fire and two of the leaders of the riot were killed, one falling across Bennett's unconscious form. Two other rioters died, and twenty more were wounded.

All over the country, the press attacked Dearborn police and the Ford Motor Company. "The Dearborn police are to be condemned for using guns against an unarmed crowd, for viciously bad judgment and for the killing of four men," said the New York *Herald Tribune*.[9]

In 1932, Hoover lost the presidency to Franklin Delano Roosevelt, who promised a "New Deal" to the American people. He used card-playing language to signify that businessmen, farmers, and working-men would now be dealt a better quality of life.

During Roosevelt's first hundred days in office, many bills were passed to help relieve the economic and social problems in the country. Things slowly began to improve, but Ford's labor troubles were only beginning.

10

LABOR PROBLEMS

In the early 1930s, labor concerns became very important in the United States. Labor laws were passed and unions became stronger.

Henry Ford believed he was a kind and generous employer and thought his employees had no need of a labor union. The Ford factories were among the cleanest, brightest, and best-ventilated factories in the country. Five thousand men with mops and buckets worked all day keeping the Rouge plant sparkling clean. There was even a special mechanism to suction the iron dust from the air when they were making piston rings.[1]

Although the factories were up-to-date and clean,

the atmosphere was terrible. Workers constantly worried about whether they would have a job. Foremen could fire people at will.

Sorensen's men constantly drove the laborers to work faster and produce more. Harry Bennett ran everything at the Rouge. Bennett's title was director of personnel, but he did anything Henry Ford wanted done, often employing violence. Ford once told him to take care of a man who had threatened one of Edsel's sons. The man was later found floating facedown in the river.[2]

Ford had hired the former sailor and boxer years before, and they had become closer through the years. Henry Ford said he liked Bennett because "Harry gets things done."[3] The employees hated and feared him. Bennett had underworld connections and did not mind using them. Ford liked the idea that Bennett was able to protect the grandchildren.

Bennett's system of spies throughout the plant reported everything to him. Walter Reuther said,

> The Rouge was a jungle because of one man, Harry Bennett. His gangsters ran that company. Harry Bennett was a mean man, a neurotic man, a man with a gangster mentality. It was absolutely fantastic that a man like that could reach the position he did with a great company like Ford.[4]

Sorensen hated Bennett, but had to work with him. Edsel hated him, too. In his memoirs, Bennett claimed, "During the thirty years I worked for

Henry Ford, I became his most intimate companion, closer to him even than his only son."[5]

Bennett admitted in his book that Edsel was his prime target. "He was a nervous man," he said, "When he got angry he threw up. He was just a scared boy as long as I knew him. Mr. Ford blamed himself for this. He had always overprotected Edsel."[6]

A short, stocky man with hard blue eyes, Bennett kept live lions and tigers as pets at his home and liked to take target practice in his office, shooting at things with his pistol. He was tough and fearless, and he ruled the Rouge.

Most Ford employees were miserable during this time. Men contracted a disease known as "Forditis."[7] They got the shakes and developed ulcers. They were afraid to speak aloud on the job.

Unions looked good to the Ford employees. However, if they admitted that, Bennett's thugs beat them up, either on the job or at home.

In July 1935, the National Labor Relations Act gave unions the right of collective bargaining. Now representatives of management had to meet with labor representatives to discuss grievances. The day the bill was signed, Henry Ford said, "We know that President Roosevelt wants to do the right and helpful thing, but I doubt if the government knows how to run a business."[8]

The National Industrial Recovery Act had also

been passed. Under this act, industries were to set minimum prices for their goods and minimum wages for their employees. This kept them from lowering prices, then lowering wages to make up for the loss. Ford refused to sign NIRA's automotive agreement. He thought he already did more for his employees than was required by this code. "I have never bargained with my men. I have always bargained for them," he said.[9]

At first, the American Federation of Labor (AFL) was the only union. It was made up mostly of skilled workers, including masons, electricians, and carpenters. In 1935, the Congress for Industrial Organization (CIO) was formed. It was made up of unskilled factory workers, under the leadership of John L. Lewis. One group in the CIO was the United Auto Workers (UAW).

The UAW was admitted into the General Motors plant, then Chrysler. Now the union set its sights on Ford Motor Company. In May 1937, they got permission from the Dearborn City Council to hand out pamphlets at the main gates of the Rouge on May 16.

Bennett and his men were prepared when the UAW representatives appeared. Walter Reuther, who had been fired from Ford for trying to get the union in, was one of the leaders, along with Richard Frankensteen and two others.

An overpass connected the parking lot to the factory across the street. The union men started across the overpass and were attacked by Bennett's thugs. Reuther felt a sharp crack across the back of his head and went down. He was dragged to his feet, beaten, thrown down, and then picked up again. He counted eight times this happened, with the attackers kicking him whenever he was down.[10]

Frankensteen's attackers pulled his coat up over his head so he could not see or move, while they kicked and beat him. Another man, Richard Merriweather, had his back broken. When Bennett's men were finished, they dragged the bleeding men to the end of the overpass and dumped them down the thirty-nine steels steps leading down to the parking lot. Reuther recalled, "The end of my spine hit every one."[11]

Reporters and photographers were on hand. Bennett's men snatched the reporters' notes and smashed the photographers' cameras. One photographer dropped his camera over the edge of the overpass into an open convertible, which drove off, preserving a record of the assault. The photographs were printed all over the world.

Ford denied his role in the whole incident.[12] Edsel had wanted to negotiate with the union. His father had told him to keep out of it, saying Bennett would handle the whole thing. The union brought

charges against Ford through the National Labor Relations Board. In February 1941, the suits were upheld in court.

On April 1, Bennett fired eight workers for union activities. Fifteen hundred others supported them by refusing to work. The strike spread to the other buildings and early that afternoon Walter Reuther made the strike official. Bennett had a group of strikebreakers ready to work in place of the strikers, but his plans backfired. These men smuggled in alcohol, got drunk, and ran races through the plant in the new cars.[13]

On the third day, Edsel convinced his father to negotiate. Bennett said later, "Mr. Ford gave in to Edsel's wishes. I don't think the CIO would have won out if it hadn't been for Edsel's attitude."[14]

The men returned to work after Ford agreed to hold an election to decide who would represent the workers. The men had three choices: the AFL, the CIO, or no union. Ford was naive enough to believe that out of gratitude to him, the workers would vote to be a nonunion shop.[15] Only 2.7 percent of the men voted that way. The CIO got 69.9 percent of the votes, making them the bargaining agent for Ford employees.

When the contract was negotiated, Ford agreed to very generous terms. They would pay back wages to over four thousand workers who had been fired due to siding with the union. Ford also matched the highest pay rate in the industry and agreed to deduct union dues from the employees' wages. Bennett's service department workers would have to wear badges or uniforms to identify themselves to the men. Now they could no longer spy for Bennett.

When Ford saw the terms the night before, he wanted to reject them, since it looked like a complete surrender. Clara told him if he did not sign the contract, she would leave him. She had had enough of bloodshed and violence.

"What could I do? . . ." Henry Ford said later. "Don't ever discredit the power of a woman."[16]

The agreement was signed on June 19, 1941, with Edsel announcing, "We have decided to go the whole way."[17]

Henry Ford in his later years

11

THE LATER
YEARS

On Ford's seventy-fifth birthday in 1938, Adolf
Hitler had awarded him the Grand Cross of
the German Eagle because of his contribution to
mass production. He could not understand the out-
rage caused by his acceptance.[1] Soon after his
birthday, Ford had suffered a slight stroke that
made him more eccentric and harder to deal with.

After Hitler's invasion of Poland in 1939, Ford
had opposed sending aid to Europe. "If we start
shipping that stuff over there, we'll be in a war right
away," he said.[2] He had read reports of a phony war
and agreed with them. "The whole thing has just
been made up by the Jew bankers," he insisted.[3]

In an about-face on May 28, 1940, Ford said his company was ready to "swing into a production of a thousand airplanes of standard design a day."[4] This was not feasible. Even plants set up for manufacturing aircraft did not come close to that figure.

In June 1940, Edsel Ford conferred with William Knudsen in Washington about manufacturing Rolls Royce Merlin aircraft engines. Knudsen, Edsel, and Sorensen were enthusiastic, and Henry Ford agreed to manufacture six thousand of the engines.

Edsel announced the project to the media. Then his father, upon learning the engines would go to England, refused to make them. He had hated England since Winston Churchill had ridiculed his advice. Ford had told Churchill that most of England's problems could be solved if farming were revolutionalized. Nothing Knudsen, Sorensen, or Edsel could say would change his mind. Edsel had the embarrassing task of announcing that Ford would not take the contract after all.

This was just one more example of Henry Ford undermining Edsel's power as president of the company. At seventy-seven he still wanted to run things, but his judgment was not as good as it had been before his stroke two years earlier.

In December 1940, the government asked Ford to build twelve hundred B-24 bombers. Sorensen,

Edsel, and his two older boys, Henry II and Benson, flew to California to look over the aircraft plants there. The boys, ages twenty-three and twenty-one, had been working for several months at the Ford plant.

They found the planes were custom made. Sorensen believed planes could be mass-produced and sketched out a plan for a plant to do just that.

Ford agreed to build a factory that could turn out a bomber an hour, if the Air Force would spend $200 million on the plant and equipment. In late February 1941, the Army authorized them to build the factory.

Ground was broken for the Willow Run plant near Ypsilanti, Michigan, on April 18, 1941. The huge L-shaped building contained a mile-long assembly line. Limited production of parts began in November. Meanwhile, Henry II, now married with a new baby, was drafted. He went into the Navy and was stationed at the Great Lakes Naval Training School.

On December 7, with the Japanese bombing of Pearl Harbor, the United States was plunged into war. On January 13, the Ford Motor Company went to a twenty-four-hour, seven-day workweek.

The same day, Edsel checked into the hospital for surgery on his stomach ulcers. Seventeen days later he was back at his desk, putting in twelve to

sixteen hours a day. Henry Ford refused to believe there was anything seriously wrong with Edsel. He thought if Edsel would just watch his diet and stay away from that fast-living Grosse Pointe crowd, he would be fine.[5] Henry thought the residents of Grosse Pointe were too snobby. In reality, Edsel lived a very quiet life.

Edsel was now drinking a lot of milk to help his stomach, and Henry Ford had some fresh milk sent over from his farms. Edsel contracted undulant fever from the unpasteurized milk. It caused excruciating pain, extreme weakness, and fits of sweating. Doctors nowadays would treat it with antibiotics, but all they could do then was prescribe rest. And with the Ford Company in the midst of defense contracts, Edsel could not do that.

By now, Harry Bennett had gotten rid of most of the top executives and replaced them with his men. He continued to badger Edsel, who became paler and weaker.

Meanwhile, his father was also failing. Henry Ford's memory was poor and he made unreasonable demands. People hoped Edsel would soon take over. Said Harold Hicks, the engineer who had developed the Model A engine, "You always figured . . . that some day he was going to run the place, and that it would be a fine place to work when he was running it. You stuck around because of him."[6]

On April 15, 1943, Henry Ford called Sorensen and told him to "change his [Edsel's] attitude on everything."[7] When Sorensen showed Edsel the list of demands from his father, he burst into tears. "The best thing for me to do is resign," Edsel said, "My health won't let me go on."[8]

Sorensen talked him out of it, saying, "If you go, I go too."[9] Edsel knew that without him and Sorensen, the Ford Motor Company would be run by a senile old man and Bennett and his group of thugs.

By now, Edsel had been diagnosed with cancer, which had spread from his stomach to his liver. He was so weak that he was on painkillers and sedatives. He came to work, but spent much of his time lying on a leather couch in his private washroom.

He finally took to his bed. The doctors did not take him to the hospital, because they knew they could do nothing for him. Henry Ford still denied his son's illness. "You know, Edsel's not going to die," he kept insisting.[10]

On May 26, 1943, Edsel Ford passed away in his bedroom at the age of forty-nine. The next day, Henry Ford called Sorensen and told him he would step back into the presidency. Sorensen could hardly believe it.[11] Ford was almost eighty years old, and getting confused.

Ford later told an old employee who had known Edsel since he was a boy, "I just can't get over it. I've

Remembering Edsel

After Edsel's funeral, Clara Ford asked Rankin, the chauffeur, to go back and get her an orchid from the coffin as a remembrance. Henry Ford seemed dazed at the funeral, and afterwards muttered, "Well, there's nothing to do. Just work harder. Work harder."[12]

got a lump right here in my throat. Clara sits down and cries and gets over it, feels a little better. I just cannot do it. I have a lump here and there's nothing I can do about it."[13]

Everyone wondered what would happen to Ford Motor Company now. Bennett was afraid Sorensen would try to take over. At this time, Ford agreed to a codicil to his will, which was a secret from the family. It set up a board to run the company for ten years after his death. None of the grandchildren were listed on the board. I. A. Capizzi, the lawyer who drew it up, said he never talked directly with Ford, but got all his information from Bennett.[14]

On June 1, 1943, the stockholders held a meeting, reelecting Henry, Henry II, and Benson Ford, as well as Sorensen, as directors. Edsel's widow, Eleanor Ford, also became a member of the board. Ray Rausch, one of Bennett's close friends, was elected, too.

Ernest Kanzler, Edsel's brother-in-law and close friend, was concerned about what would become of the company Edsel had given his life for. He arranged with Secretary of the Navy Frank Knox for Henry II to be released from the Navy to help.

Henry Ford went on vacation instead of staying to greet his grandson when he came home. Young Henry II moved into his father's office. "I didn't have a job," he said. "Nobody had any suggestion as to what I might do, so I just moseyed around on my own, visited the plants, talked with the fellows, trying to find out how things operated."[15]

Sorensen later wrote, "Wherever this 25-year-old young man went he, too, made an impression—a good one."[16] Henry II did not care for Sorensen and his methods, but he could work with him. He stayed away from Bennett as much as possible.

Henry II was mild-mannered and modest like his father, but he had his grandfather's tenacity. He found the plant was grossly mismanaged.

Bennett was always conniving to have things his way. Henry II later recalled,

> When an important policy matter came up, Bennett would get into his car and disappear for a few hours. Then he'd come back and say, "I've been to see Mr. Ford and he wants us to do it this way." I checked with my grandfather and found out that Bennett hadn't seen my grandfather on those occasions.[17]

He knew it would not do any good to complain about Bennett to his grandfather. According to Henry Ford, Bennett could do no wrong. Soon after Edsel died, a man from *Reader's Digest* asked Ford who was the greatest man he had ever met. Ford immediately answered, "Harry Bennett."[18]

Ford began spending much of his time at Greenfield Village. The chauffeur took him to the Mary-Martha Chapel (a memorial to his and Clara's mothers) each morning, so he could hear the children sing hymns. Often he sat on the grass under a tree and played his Jew's harp, a small lyre-shaped instrument, for the children who gathered around.

While his grandfather wandered around the Village, Henry II was hard at work, trying to straighten out the mess at the plant. Bennett saw Sorensen as a threat to his power. Although Sorensen's methods were not always pleasant, he was honest and had always worked for the good of the company. He knew Bennett was manipulating Henry Ford, and he knew his job was in danger. Bennett had appointed himself as Sorensen's assistant.

Finally, on January 1, Sorensen left for Florida. He said later that before he left, he had advised Ford to make Henry II president without delay. In March, Sorensen, who had been with Ford Motor Company since 1905, received a message from

Henry Ford asking for his resignation. Ford said he was trying to get the presidency of the company.[19]

Sorensen resigned, and now it was a showdown between Bennett and Henry II. "I didn't know how secure I was," Henry II later said.[20] He had some advantages, though. Most employees thought he would one day be the boss. Young Henry's mother, grandmother, and brothers were solidly behind him. And war production leaders in Washington had no faith in Bennett.

Clara finally decided she had to interfere in her husband's affairs in order to help her grandson. She tried to convince her husband the time had come to transfer the presidency to Henry II. He was reluctant to do it until Eleanor Ford gave an ultimatum. "If this is not done," she said, "I shall sell my stock!"[21] Ford gave in.

He called Henry II to Fair Lane and told him he was ready for him to take over. "I told him I'd take it only if I had a completely free hand to make any changes I wanted to make," Henry II later said. "We argued about that—but he didn't withdraw his offer."[22]

Several sources state that young Henry received a phone call from Bennett before the special board meeting called for the next day. "I've got wonderful news for you," he said. "I've just talked your grandfather into making you president of the company."[23]

Bennett was not that pleasant at the meeting, though. As soon as the letter was read, he got up, barked "Congratulations" at Henry II, and started to leave.[24] He was prevailed upon to stay until the vote was taken. Henry II was elected president.

His first act as president of Ford Motor Company was to walk down the hall to Bennett's office and fire him. He recalled that meeting. "Bennett seemed in a state of shock—in a daze. I simply said to him, 'Harry, we've got to part company.' Then I told him I'd keep him on salary for a year and a half until his retirement pay would begin."[25]

Bennett had to have the last word. "You're taking over a billion dollar organization here that you haven't contributed a thing to!"[26] Bennett spent the afternoon burning documents, and left the next day for California.

As things began looking better at the plant under the direction of Henry II, his grandfather continued to go downhill. He and Clara spent February and March of 1947 at their winter home in Richmond Hill, Georgia. They arrived home on April 6.

There had been a lot of rain, and the next morning, they received a phone call that the power plant was submerged, so they would not have any electricity or heat. Henry Ford laughed at the suggestion that they go to the Dearborn Inn for breakfast. "My gracious," he said. "We have

In 1945, Henry Ford II (left) became president of Ford Motor Company.

fireplaces! In Scotland or in Ireland they cook everything on the fireplace!"[27]

After a breakfast cooked in the fireplace, he
asked Rankin to drive him around to see the flood

damage. They went to Greenfield Village, and then stopped at the little family cemetery on Joy Road. "Rankin, this is where I'm going to be buried when I die," he told the chauffeur.[28]

Henry and Clara Ford retired early that night, but he woke her up at 11:15, complaining of a bad headache and a dry throat. The phone was out, so Clara sent Rankin to get the doctor. She and her maid, Rosa Buhler, stayed with Mr. Ford. "What do you think?" Clara asked the maid.[29]

Rosa replied, "I think Mr. Ford will be leaving us."[30]

She was right. By the time Dr. Mateer arrived, a little after midnight, Henry Ford had died, three months short of his eighty-fourth birthday. Henry II and his wife, Anne, came straight from the train station, where they had just arrived from New York. Clara also sent for their mutual friend Evangeline Dahlinger to say her farewells.[31]

Henry Ford's body lay in state on April 9 in the Recreation Hall in his beloved Greenfield Village. The next day, twenty thousand people gathered in the rain outside St. Paul's Episcopal Cathedral in Detroit. The City Hall was draped in black, and a thirty-foot portrait of Henry Ford hung there. When the service started at 2:30 P.M., all of Detroit came to a halt for a minute to remember the man and his contributions to Detroit and the world.

The Legacy of Henry Ford

More than anything else, Henry Ford was a man of contradictions. For every facet of his personality, there was an opposite trait.

When the Ford Motor Company began in 1903, Ford spent time in the plant, talking to the workers and encouraging them. This was a far cry from his inhumane treatment of employees at the Rouge in the 1930s. Much of this change can be attributed to the influence of Harry Bennett.

Henry Ford's relationship with his wife, Clara, was another contradiction. They seemed perfectly matched and got along well for the almost fifty-nine years of their marriage. However, Ford spent many

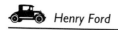

hours with Ray and Evangeline Dahlinger and their son, John, said to be Ford's illegitimate son. Much evidence points to this being true. Ford appeared in the hospital nursery immediately after the baby was born. He hired the nurse who was taking care of him to go home with the Dahlingers and serve as a full-time nurse to the child.

Ford bought the Dahlingers a huge mansion, land, horses, and much more. He spent a lot of time with young John, lavishing gifts on him, including a Shetland pony when he was one month old. He insist-ed John sleep in the cradle he himself had slept in as a baby. He was very involved in the boy's education.

As an adult, John Dahlinger bore an amazing resemblance to Edsel Ford. When he asked his mother if Ford was his biological father, she refused to discuss it, which convinced him it was true. Clara Ford sent for Evangeline to say her last good-byes after Henry Ford died.[1]

Ford's attitude toward Edsel was equally contra-dictory. He spent many hours with the child, playing with him, photographing him, and writing letters to him when he was away. It was unusual at the time for a father to be that close to a child. Women did most of the child care and men worked to bring in money. As Edsel grew older and began to help at the plant, his father was very proud of him and the two were extremely close.

However, as Bennett's influence increased, so did the distance between father and son. Eleanor Ford blamed her father-in-law and Harry Bennett for her husband's early death.[2] The root of the problem was Henry Ford's desire for Edsel to be a carbon copy of him.

Ford did not believe in charity, and he was seemingly very callous toward his employees at times. He displayed indifference toward much of the suffering during the Depression, yet he put the village of Inkster back on its feet through his generosity. Inkster was a struggling village near Detroit. Ford opened a commissary where the townspeople could use IOU's to purchase food. He built a school, gave hospital care to the sick, and repaired the streets. He created jobs by setting up a clinic, tailor shop, dressmaking shop, bakery, and shoe-repair shop.

The Ford Foundation, set up as a shelter from taxes in 1935, grew to be one of the major philanthropic foundations in the country after Ford's death.

Even Ford's much-publicized stand on peace was contradictory. He did not believe in war because it was violent, yet he allowed, and even approved, all manner of violence carried out by Bennett. He stated he would rather burn down his factory than manufacture goods for the war effort, and then he did an about-face. The Peace Ship, although a failure in the eyes of many, was an honest attempt to bring about world peace.

Henry Ford did make many positive contributions to his country and the world. He did not invent the first car. Several others built cars before him. He did, however, make the automobile available and affordable for the average workingman.

Others used elements of the assembly line before he did, but the Ford factory was the first to assemble a complete automobile on the assembly line. They really perfected the technique with the Model T.

Henry Ford, who once said history was mostly bunk (nonsense), may have done more than any other man to preserve the history of nineteenth- and twentieth-century America. His village on the site of the Wayside Inn in Massachusetts was the first functional restored village in the country. Greenfield Village and the Henry Ford Museum have over a million visitors a year. The Village shows how people lived during the earlier days of our country while the museum showcases technological and cultural accomplishments. Henry Ford's own accomplishments number among the most important of the twentieth century, ensuring that as long as there are automobiles, he will not be forgotten.

CHRONOLOGY

1863—*July 30:* Born in Dearbornville, Michigan.

1876—Ford's mother dies.

1879—Goes to Detroit to work at age sixteen.

1882—Moves back to the farm in Dearborn.

1888—*April 11:* Marries Clara Jane Bryant.

1891—Moves back to Detroit to work at Edison Illuminating Company.

1893—*November 6:* Son, Edsel Ford, is born.

1895—Builds the Quadricycle, his first successful automobile.

1899—Detroit Automobile Company is formed.

1901—Detroit Automobile Company is dissolved; Henry Ford Company is formed and dissolved.

1903—Ford Motor Company is formed; First Ford automobile is sold; Association of Licensed Automobile Manufacturers files suit against Ford Motor Company for infringement of Selden patent.

1908—Model T is introduced.

1910—Highland Park plant goes into operation.

1911—Selden patent suit is settled in Ford's favor.

1913—Moving assembly line is introduced.

1914—Wages are raised to five dollars a day at Ford's plant.

1915—Takes Peace Ship to Europe to try to settle World War I.

1916—Edsel Ford marries Eleanor Clay; Dodge brothers file suit against Ford Motor Company; Henry Ford files libel suit against Chicago *Tribune*.

1918—Makes unsuccessful run for the Senate.

1919—Loses Dodge suit; Launches the *Dearborn Independent;* Wins suit against *Tribune;* Resigns as president of Ford Motor Company; Edsel Ford is named president.

1920—River Rouge plant opens; Attacks against Jews launched in *Dearborn Independent.*

1927—Model A is introduced.

1929—Greenfield Village opens.

1932—V-8 engine is introduced in Ford automobiles; Hunger March is staged by Communists.

1935—National Labor Relations Act is passed.

1937—Battle of the Overpass between United Auto Workers (UAW) representatives and Ford Motor Company at the Rouge.

1941—UAW wins election to represent Ford employees.

1943—*May 26:* Edsel Ford dies; Henry Ford steps back into presidency of company.

1945—Henry Ford II becomes president of Ford Motor Company.

1947—*April 7:* Henry Ford dies at Dearborn, Michigan.

CHAPTER NOTES

Chapter 1. Testing the Quadricycle

1. James Brough, *The Ford Dynasty* (Garden City, N.Y.: Doubleday and Co., 1977), p. 44.

2. Allan Nevins and Frank Hill, *Ford: The Times, The Man, The Company* (New York: Charles Scribner's Sons, 1954), p. 157.

3. William A. Simonds, *Henry Ford: His Life—His Work—His Genius* (Indianapolis, Ind.: The Bobbs-Merrill Company, 1943), p. 53.

Chapter 2. Henry Ford, Farm Boy

1. Peter Collier and David Horowitz, *The Fords: An American Epic* (New York: Summit Books, 1987), p. 18.

2. William A. Simonds, *Henry Ford: His Life—His Work—His Genius* (Indianapolis, Ind.: The Bobbs-Merrill Company, 1943), p. 26.

3. Allan Nevins and Frank Hill, *Ford: The Times, The Man, The Company* (New York: Charles Scribner's Sons, 1954), p. 42.

4. James Brough, *The Ford Dynasty* (Garden City, N.Y.: Doubleday and Co., 1977), p. 32.

5. Robert Lacey, *Ford: The Men and the Machine* (Boston: Little, Brown and Company, 1986), p. 11.

6. Simonds, p. 26.

7. Nevins and Hill, p. 45.

8. Ibid.

9. Ibid., p. 47.

10. Brough, p. 33.

11. Nevins and Hill, p. 48.

12. Ibid.

13. Ibid.

14. Brough, p. 33.

15. Lacey, p. 11.

16. Nevins and Hill, p. 52.

17. Lacey, pp. 12–13.

18. Ibid.

19. Nevins and Hill, p. 55.

20. Lacey, p. 11.

21. Brough, p. 36.

22. Ibid.

23. Lacey, p. 15.

Chapter 3. Independence and Marriage

1. Robert Lacey, *Ford: The Men and the Machine* (Boston: Little, Brown and Company, 1986), p. 16.

2. James Brough, *The Ford Dynasty* (Garden City, N.Y.: Doubleday and Co., 1977), pp. 37–38.

3. Lacey, p. 17.

4. William A. Simonds, *Henry Ford: His Life—His Work—His Genius* (Indianapolis, Ind.: The Bobbs-Merrill Company, 1943), p. 38.

5. Ibid., p. 39.

6. Peter Collier and David Horowitz, *The Fords: An American Epic* (New York: Summit Books, 1987), p. 26.

7. Lacey, p. 30.

Chapter 4. Race Cars and Business Failures

1. Carol Gelderman, *Henry Ford: The Wayward Capitalist* (New York: The Dial Press, 1981), p. 17.

2. Regina Z. Kelly, *Henry Ford* (New York: Follett Publishing Company, 1970), p. 40.

3. Ibid., p. 46.

4. Allan Nevins and Frank Hill, *Ford: The Times, The Man, The Company* (New York: Charles Scribner's Sons, 1954), p. 161.

5. Peter Collier and David Horowitz, *The Fords: An American Epic* (New York: Summit Books, 1987), p. 33.

6. Nevins and Hill, p. 180.

7. Ibid., p. 184.

8. James Brough, *The Ford Dynasty* (Garden City, N.Y.: Doubleday and Co., 1977), p. 51.

9. Ibid.

10. Collier and Horowitz, p. 41.

11. Brough, p. 56.

12. Collier and Horowitz, p. 43.

Chapter 5. Ford Pioneers the Assembly Line

1. Keith Sward, *The Legacy of Henry Ford* (New York: Rinehart, 1948), p. 20.

2. Carol Gelderman, *Henry Ford: The Wayward Capitalist* (New York: The Dial Press, 1981), p. 35.

3. Sward, p. 30.

4. Allan Nevins and Frank Hill, *Ford: The Times, The Man, The Company* (New York: Charles Scribner's Sons, 1954), p. 296.

5. Ibid., p. 297.

6. Ibid., p. 301.

7. Regina Z. Kelly, *Henry Ford* (New York: Follett Publishing Company, 1970), p. 84.

8. Ibid., p. 76.

9. Robert Lacey, *Ford: The Men and the Machine* (Boston: Little, Brown and Company, 1986), p. 91.

10. Ibid.

11. Kelly, p. 81.

12. Ibid., p. 91.

13. James Brough, *The Ford Dynasty* (Garden City, N.Y.: Doubleday and Co., 1977), p. 72.

14. Lacey, p. 101.

15. Gelderman, p. 46.

16. Brough, p. 63.

17. Ibid., p. 76.

18. Gelderman, p. 47.

19. Lacey, p. 109.

20. Ibid.

21. Kelly, p. 90.

22. Sward, p. 52.

23. Ibid., p. 53.

24. Gelderman, p. 55.

25. Lacey, p. 122.

Chapter 6. The Peace Ship

1. Robert Lacey, *Ford: The Men and the Machine* (Boston: Little, Brown and Company, 1986), p. 134.

2. Regina Z. Kelly, *Henry Ford* (New York: Follett Publishing Company, 1970), p. 115.

3. Lacey, p. 133.

4. Burnet Hershey, *The Odyssey of Henry Ford: The Great Peace Ship* (New York: Taplinger Publishing Company, 1967), p. 16.

5. Louis Paul Lochner, *Henry Ford: America's Don Quixote* (New York: International Publishers, 1925), p. 24.

6. Ibid.

7. Ibid.

8. James Brough, *The Ford Dynasty* (Garden City, N.Y.: Doubleday and Co., 1977), p. 23.

9. Lochner, p. 27.

10. Lacey, p. 139.

11. Ibid.

12. Carol Gelderman, *Henry Ford: The Wayward Capitalist* (New York: The Dial Press, 1981), p. 101.

13. Lochner, p. 38.

14. Keith Sward, *The Legacy of Henry Ford* (New York: Rinehart, 1948), p. 88.

15. Ibid.

16. Ibid.

17. Gelderman, p. 109.

18. Sward, p. 88.

19. Lacey, p. 142.

20. Gelderman, p. 117.

21. Ibid.

22. Ibid., p. 119.

23. Kelly, p. 111.

24. Gelderman, p. 120.

25. Sward, p. 91.

26. Brough, p. 24.

27. Gelderman, p. 127.

28. Ibid.

Chapter 7. War, Trials, and Retirement

1. Robert Lacey, *Ford: The Men and the Machine* (Boston: Little, Brown and Company, 1986), p. 197.

2. Allan Nevins and Frank Hill, *Ford: Expansion and Challenge: 1915–1933* (New York: Charles Scribner's Sons, 1957), p. 130.

3. Ibid.

4. Allan Nevins and Frank Hill, *Ford: The Times, The Man, The Company* (New York: Charles Scribner's Sons, 1954). p. 584.

5. Regina Z. Kelly, *Henry Ford* (New York: Follett Publishing Company, 1970), p. 115.

6. Lacey, p. 152.

7. Ibid.

8. Keith Sward, *The Legacy of Henry Ford* (New York: Rinehart, 1948), p. 94.

9. Lacey, p. 156.

10. Ibid.

11. Sward, p. 96.

12. Lacey, p. 159.

13. Sward, p. 95.

14. James Brough, *The Ford Dynasty* (Garden City, N.Y.: Doubleday and Co., 1977), p. 99.

15. Nevins and Hill, *Expansion,* p. 118.

16. Ibid.

17. Carol Gelderman, *Henry Ford: The Wayward Capitalist* (New York: The Dial Press, 1981), p. 146.

18. Ibid., p. 150.

19. Nevins and Hill, *Expansion,* p. 119.

20. Lacey, p. 176.

21. Ibid., p. 177.

Chapter 8. Greenfield Village and the Henry Ford Museum

1. Geoffrey C. Upward, *A Home for Our Heritage: The Building and Growth of Greenfield Village and Henry Ford Museum, 1929–1979* (Dearborn, Mich.: The Henry Ford Museum Press, 1979), p. 3.

2. Ibid., p. 8.

3. Ibid.

4. Ibid., p. 12.

5. Ibid., p. 3.

6. Ibid., p. 28.

7. Ibid., p. 22.

8. Ibid., p. 60.

Chapter 9. The Twenties, the Thirties, and the Great Depression

1. William A. Simonds, *Henry Ford: His Life—His Work—His Genius* (Indianapolis, Ind.: The Bobbs-Merrill Company, 1943), p. 349.

2. John Dahlinger, *The Secret Life of Henry Ford* (Indianapolis, Ind.: The Bobbs-Merrill Company, 1978), p. 107.

3. James Brough, *The Ford Dynasty* (Garden City, N.Y.: Doubleday and Co., 1977), p. 175.

4. Booten Herndon, *Ford: An Unconventional Biography of the Men and their Times* (New York: Weybright and Talley, 1969), p. 155.

5. Charles Merz, *And Then Came Ford* (Garden City, N.Y.: Doubleday, Doran and Company, Inc., 1929), p. 300.

6. Robert Lacey, *Ford: The Men and the Machine* (Boston: Little, Brown and Company, 1986), p. 311.

7. Ibid., p. 312.

8. Simonds, p. 229.

9. Robert Lacey, p. 344.

Chapter 10. Labor Problems

1. Robert Lacey, *Ford: The Men and the Machine* (Boston: Little, Brown and Company, 1986), p. 350.

2. Peter Collier and David Horowitz, *The Fords: An American Epic* (New York: Summit Books, 1987), p. 151.

3. Allen Nevins and Frank Hill, *Ford: Expansion and Challenge, 1915–1933* (New York: Charles Scribner's Sons, 1957), p. 591.

4. Booten Herndon, *Ford: An Unconventional Biography of the Men and their Times* (New York: Weybright and Talley, 1969), p. 156.

5. William A. Simonds, *Henry Ford: His Life—His Work—His Genius* (Indianapolis, Ind.: The Bobbs-Merrill Company, 1943), p. 379.

6. Herndon, p. 157.

7. Ibid., p. 171.

8. Regina C. Kelly, *Henry Ford* (New York: Follett Publishing Company, 1970), p. 162.

9. Ibid.

10. Lacey, p. 356.

11. Ibid.

12. Herndon, p. 173.

13. Lacey, p. 376.

14. Herndon, p. 174.

15. Lacey, p. 377.

16. Ibid., p. 378.

17. James Brough, *The Ford Dynasty* (Garden City, N.Y.: Doubleday and Co., 1977), p. 215.

Chapter 11. The Later Years

1. William A. Simonds, *Henry Ford: His Life—His Work—His Genius* (Indianapolis, Ind.: The Bobbs-Merrill Company, 1943), p. 285.

2. Robert Lacey, *Ford: The Men and the Machine* (Boston: Little, Brown and Company, 1986), p. 386.

3. Ibid., p. 387.

4. Ibid.

5. James Brough, *The Ford Dynasty* (Garden City, N.Y.: Doubleday and Co., 1977), p. 217.

6. Lacey, p. 394.

7. Ibid., p. 396.

8. Ibid.

9. Ibid.

10. Brough, p. 218.

11. Ibid.

12. Ibid.

13. Peter Collier and David Horowitz, *The Fords: An American Epic* (New York: Summit Books, 1987), p. 191.

14. Allan Nevins and Frank Hill, *Ford: Decline and Rebirth: 1933–1962* (New York: Charles Scriber's Sons, 1962), p. 249.

15. Brough, p. 221.

16. Lacey, p. 254.

17. Ibid., p. 256.

18. Brough, p. 219.

19. Nevins and Hill, p. 260.

20. Ibid., p. 263.

21. Ibid., p. 268.

22. Brough, p. 237.

23. Ibid.

24. Nevins and Hill, p. 269.

25. Brough, p. 238.

26. Nevins and Hill, p. 269.

27. Lacey, p. 456.

28. Brough, p. 250.

29. Lacey, p. 447.

30. Ibid.

31. Ibid.

Chapter 12. The Legacy of Henry Ford

1. Robert Lacey, *Ford: The Men and the Machine* (Boston: Little, Brown and Company, 1986), pp. 183–193.

2. Ibid., p. 143.

GLOSSARY

American Federation of Labor (AFL)—A national labor union, made up mostly of craftsmen.

anarchist—A person who does not believe in organized government.

apprentice—Someone who works for low wages for several years in order to learn a trade.

assembly line—An arrangement in a factory where each worker does one small job or puts on one part as the product moves past.

Congress of Industrial Organizations (CIO)—A labor union made up of industrial workers.

chassis—The frame of an automobile.

Dearborn Independent—A newspaper started by Henry Ford to express his opinions.

dividends—A share of profits of a company that is divided among stockholders.

Eagle boats—Boats manufactured by Ford Motor Company for the Navy Department during World War I.

Ford Foundation—A foundation that donates money in order to help people help themselves.

Great Depression—A period, from 1929 through the time the United States entered World War II, when many people were out of work and many banks and businesses failed.

guerrillas—Soldiers who make surprise raids, often behind enemy lines.

Hunger March—A protest against Ford Motor Company, organized by the Communists.

Independence Hall—A building in Philadelphia where the Liberty Bell is displayed.

infringement—Violation.

Kaiser Wilhelm—The ruler of Germany during World War I.

League of Nations—An organization, similar to the United Nations. It was established at the end of World War I to help establish international cooperation and peace. The United States never joined.

libel—A false or malicious printed statement.

The National Labor Relations Act (NLRA)—An act which granted employees the right to negotiate with management.

pacifist—A person who is opposed to the use of force, especially in war.

Peace Ship—A ship, the *Oscar II*, which Henry Ford took to Europe during World War I in an attempt to negotiate peace with the warring nations.

Potato Famine—A time in the late 1840s when many people in Ireland starved because the potato crops failed for several years in a row.

preparedness—The U.S. policy of preparing for war, even though the country was neutral.

Quadricycle—Henry Ford's first automobile, made with four bicycle wheels.

stockholders—People who own shares in a company and receive dividends when it makes a profit.

United Auto Workers (UAW)—A division of the Congress of Industrial Organizations (CIO).

undulant fever—Illness caused by contaminated milk. Symptoms are intermittent fever, joint pain, and sweating.

V-8—An engine with eight cylinders arranged in a V-shape.

FURTHER READING

Books

Aird, Hazel B. *Henry Ford: Young Man with Ideas*. Old Tappan, N.J.: Macmillan Publishing Company.

Gould, William. *Ford*. Lincolnwood, Ill.: N.T.C. Publishing Company, 1996.

Joseph, Paul. *Henry Ford*. Minneapolis: ABDO Publishing Company, 1996.

Internet Addresses

"Henry Ford Estate: A National Historic Landmark." n.d. <http://www.umd.umich.edu/fairlane/>.

"The Henry Ford Museum & Greenfield Village." 2001. <http://www.hfmgv.org>.

Lee Iacocca. "Driving Force: Henry Ford." *Time 100: Builders & Titans*. n.d. <http://www.time.com/time/time100/builder/profile/ford.html>.

INDEX